Spain unlocked an expat's key to the real estate market

Expert, Expat Agent Nikki Powles explains the buying process in Spain

Author: Nikki Powles

Copyright © 2023 Nikki Powles

All rights reserved. No part of this book may be reproduced or transmitted in any form or by any means, electronic or mechanical, including photocopying, recording, or by any information storage and retrieval system, without permission in writing from the copyright holder.

Table of Contents

1. Introduction 1
   - My journey 1
   Moving lock stock and barrel to Spain! 1
   - Why Spain- The Allure of the Spanish Lifestyle 3
   Pace of Life: Tranquilo 4
   Cuisine and Food Culture 4
   Outdoor Living and Climate 4
   Sense of Community and Family 5
   Fiestas and Festivals 5
   Art, Music, and Culture 5
   Affordable and Quality Living 6
   Connection to Nature 6
2. Understanding Spain- Climate and Weather Patterns 7
   - Overview of Regions and Cities 7
   Andalucía 7
       Key Cities: Seville, Granada, Málaga, Córdoba, Cádiz 7
   Catalonia (Cataluña) Key Cities: Barcelona, Girona, Tarragona, Lleida 8
   Madrid (Community of Madrid) the capital 9
   Valencian Community (Comunidad Valenciana) Valencia, Alicante, Castellón de la Plana 9

Basque Country (País Vasco) Bilbao, San Sebastián, Vitoria-Gasteiz 10

Galicia Santiago de Compostela, A Coruña, Vigo 11

Castile and León (Castilla y León) Valladolid, Salamanca, León, Burgos 11

Canary Islands (Islas Canarias) Las Palmas (Gran Canaria), Santa Cruz (Tenerife) 12

Balearic Islands (Islas Baleares) Palma (Mallorca), Ibiza, Menorca 12

Mediterranean Climate (Coastal Areas: Southern and Eastern Spain) 13

    Regions: Andalucía (Costa del Sol, Costa de la Luz), Catalonia (Costa Brava), Valencia (Costa Blanca), Balearic Islands 13

Continental Climate (Inland and Central Spain) 15

    Regions: Madrid, Castile and León, Castile-La Mancha, Extremadura 15

Oceanic Climate (Northern Spain) 16

    Regions: Galicia, Asturias, Cantabria, Basque Country ... 16

Semi-Arid Climate (Southeastern Spain) 17

    Murcia, Almería, parts of Valencia and Alicante 17

Mountain Climate (Pyrenees, Sierra Nevada, and Cantabrian Mountains) 18

    Northern Spain (Pyrenees), Southern Spain (Sierra Nevada), Northwestern Spain (Cantabrian Mountains) .. 18

Subtropical Climate (Canary Islands) 19
   Regions: Canary Islands (Tenerife, Gran Canaria, Lanzarote, Fuerteventura) 19
   Overall Impact on Energy and Housing 20
- Cost of Living and Property Prices 20
Madrid: The Capital City- Cost of Living: 21
   - Property Prices: 21
   - City Center 21
   - Suburban Areas: 21
   - Other Costs: 21
Barcelona: Cosmopolitan and Costly- Cost of Living: 21
   - Property Prices: 22
   - City Center 22
Andalucía: Affordable Southern Living- Cost of Living: 22
   - Property Prices: 23
   - Seville: 23
   - Málaga: 23
   - Countryside: 23
   - Other Costs: 23
Valencian Community: A Mid-Range Option- Cost of Living: 23
   - Valencia City: 24
   - Alicante: 24

- Countryside and Smaller Towns: 24

- Other Costs: 24

Basque Country: Higher Living Costs, Strong Economy-
Cost of Living: 25

- Property Prices: 25

- Bilbao: 25

- San Sebastián: 25

- Smaller Towns: 25

- Other Costs: 25

Galicia: Budget-Friendly in the Northwest - Cost of Living:
.... 26

- Property Prices: 26

- Santiago de Compostela: 26

- A Coruña and Vigo: 26

- Countryside: 26

- Other Costs: 26

Canary Islands: - Cost of Living: 27

- Tenerife and Gran Canarian: 27

- Lanzarote and Fuerteventura: 27

- Other Costs: 27

Rural Spain: Low-Cost Countryside Living 28

- Regions: 28

Extremadura, Castilla-La Mancha, Aragón, parts of Castile and León 28

Cost of Living 28

- Property Prices: 28

Extremadura: 28

- Castilla-La Mancha: 28

- Other Costs: 28

3. The Buying Process 29

- How to Start: Research and Preparation 29

Researching Potential Locations 29

- Lifestyle Preferences: 29

- Climate: 29

- Work Opportunities or Retirement: 29

- Cultural Interests: 30

- Access to Services: 30

- Property Market Analysis: 30

Understanding the Housing Market 31

- Urban vs. Rural: 31

- Coastal vs. Inland: 31

- Rental vs. Purchase: 31

- Market Trends: 31

Setting a Budget 32

- Property Price Range: 32

- Mortgage Requirements: 32

- Additional Costs: 32

- Property Transfer Tax (ITP): 32

- Notary and Land Registry Fees: 32

- Legal Fees: 33

- Living Costs: 33

- Currency Exchange Rates: 33

Visiting Areas Before Making Decisions 33

- Firsthand Experience: 33

- Seasonal Differences: 34

- Meet with Real Estate Agents: 34

- Talk to Locals: 34

Starting the Legal and Financial Process Early 34

- Hire a Lawyer: 34

- NIE (Foreigner's Identification Number): 35

Form EX-15 (Application for NIE) 35

- Where to Download: 35

- Link to Form EX-15 (PDF): 35

- Filling Out the Form: 35

Form 790 (Tax Payment for NIE Application) 36

- Where to Download: 36

- Link to Form 790 (PDF): 36

- Filling Out the Form: 36
Where to Submit Your Application 36
- At a Spanish Police Station or Foreigners' Office: 36
- Appointment (Cita Previa): 36
Required Documents 37
- Open a Spanish Bank Account: 37
Negotiating and Making an Offer 38
- Property Surveys: 38
- Negotiation: 38
- Reservation Agreement: 38
Final Steps: Closing the Sale 39
- Private Purchase Contract: 39
- Completion: 39
Key Tips: 39
- Take Your Time: 39
- Choosing the Right Location for Your Lifestyle 40
- Understanding the Buying Process: Steps and Timeline .. 40
- Key Considerations: New Builds vs. Resales 42
Quality 42
New-Build Homes: 42
Resale Properties: 43
Timeline for Completion 44

New-Build Homes: 44

Resale Properties: 45

Taxation Differences 45

New-Build Homes: 45

Resale Properties: 46

Resale Value 46

New-Build Homes: 46

Resale Properties: 47

Financial Aspects 48

- Buying Costs: What to Expect 48

Property Transfer Taxes 48

Resale Properties: 49

Notary Fees (Notaría) 49

Land Registry Fees (Registro de la Propiedad) 49

Legal Fees (Abogado) 50

Survey Fees (Tasación) 50

Mortgage-Related Costs 50

- Mortgage Registry Fee: 51

- Bank Arrangement Fees (Comisión de Apertura): 51

Banking Costs 51

Estate Agent Fees (Agente Inmobiliario) 51

- Buyer fees: 52

- Home Insurance 52
- Utility Connection Fees 52
- Other Administrative Costs 52
- Maintenance Fees (Community Fees) 53
- Total Additional Costs Estimate: 53
- What are "AFO," "DAFO," and "SAFO" certifications? 53

Building on Rustic land 56

- Mortgages: Options and Requirements 58
- Types of Mortgages for Expats 58
- - Resident Mortgages: 58
- - Non-Resident Mortgages: 59
- Down Payment Requirements 59
- The 90 days in 180 rule 59
- The Rule: 60
- How the 180-Day Period Works: 60
- How It Impacts Travel: 61
- Consequences of Overstaying: 61

Wills in Spain 61

Visas: Types and How to Obtain Them 62
- Non-Lucrative Visa 62
- Golden Visa (Investor Visa) 63
- Work Visa/Permit 64

Self-employed Visa: 64
Entrepreneur Visa 65
Student Visa 66
Family Reunification Visa 66
Digital Nomad Visa (in progress or recently introduced in some countries, like Spain) 67

Working with Professionals 67
- Finding the Right Real Estate Agent 67
Local Knowledge and Expertise 68
Language Proficiency and Communication 68
Professional Network 69
Commitment to Transparency 70
Using MLS and Property Portals for Property Searches .. 70
Multiple Listing Services (MLS) 70
Property Portals 71
- Engaging a Lawyer: Why It's Essential 73
Ensuring Compliance with Spanish Property Law 73
Representation in Your Absence 77

Setting Up Your New Life 77
Car Hire in Spain 77
Train Services in Spain 79
- Tips for Using Trains: 79
Proximity of Airports 80

- Major Airports in Spain: 80
- Airport Transfers: 81
- Tips for Bus Travel: 82
Urban Public Transport 82
- Tips for Public Transport: 83

Living in Spain 84

- Integrating into the Community: Tips for Expats 84
Join Expat and Local Groups 84
Learn Spanish (or the Local Language) 86
- Tips for Language Learning: 86
Participate in Local Festivals and Events 87
- Tips for Festivals: 88
4. Volunteer in Your Local Community 88
Get Involved in Local Politics and Associations 89
Support Local Businesses and Markets 90
- Navigating Local Culture and Customs 90

Dining Habits 90

Siesta and Business Hours 91
Social Etiquette 92
Family and Social Life 92
Time Perception 93
Work-Life Balance 94

Language 94

Driving and Public Transport 94

- Pets and Animals: Bringing Your Furry Friends 95

Microchip and Identification 95

Vaccination Requirements 95

Health Certificate 96

Transporting Your Pet 96

Entering Spain 97

Quarantine 97

Navigating Pet-Friendly Housing in Spain 97

Accessing Pet-Friendly Areas 98

Other Considerations 98

Empadronamiento: Register with local authorities. 98

The Tarjeta de Identidad de Extranjero (TIE) 99

Steps for Applying for a TIE 100

Selling Your Property 102

- The Selling Process: From Listing to Closing 102

1. Finding a Real Estate Agent 102

- Research: 102

2. Preparing the Property for Sale 103

- Property Presentation: 104

3. Marketing the Property 104

Receiving Offers and Negotiating 105

Signing the Reservation Agreement (Contrato de Reserva) 105

Signing the Private Purchase Contract (Contrato de Arras) 106

Final Legal and Financial Preparations 106

Closing the Sale 107

Post-Sale Responsibilities 108

Final Checklist: 108

- Selling Costs: What to Consider 108

Real Estate Agent Fees 108

Capital Gains Tax (CGT) 109

Plusvalía Tax (Municipal Capital Gains Tax) 110

Non-Resident Withholding Tax 110

Legal Fees 111

Notary and Registry Fees 111

Mortgage Cancellation Fees (If Applicable) 112

Energy Performance Certificate (EPC) 112

Miscellaneous Costs 113

Example Cost Breakdown for a €300,000 Sale (Non-Resident) 113

Why Get a Spanish will? 114

- Preparing Your Home for Sale 115

Property Staging 115
- Tidy the garden and entrance: 117
Marketing the Home Effectively 119
High-Quality Photography 119
Create an Appealing Listing 120
Leverage Online Property Portals 120
Open Houses and Viewings 121
Highlight Special Selling Points 121
Bonus Tip: Competitive Pricing 121
- Your Checklist for Moving to Spain 122
1. Pre-Move Research 122
2. Legal Requirements 122
3. Financial Planning 122
4. Housing 123
5. Settling In 123
6. Building Your New Life 123
Official Government Websites 125
- Expat Rights and Regulations (EU Citizens): 125
5. Expats Forums and Communities 126
6. Local Services and Directories 127
Healthcare Providers and Insurance 127
Schools and Education 128

Curriculum Options 128

Locations and Notable Schools.. 129

Fees and Admission 130

Unique Offerings and Extracurriculars........................... 131

About the Author... 132

Other resources and My channels:..................................... 133

Disclaimer:.. 134

1. Introduction

- My journey

Moving lock stock and barrel to Spain!

24 years ago I moved my family My now Ex husband, two kids aged 3 and 6, Also 2 horses and 2 dogs to Southern Spain to a rental property we found on a 2 day exploration trip with an agent online. We had 5000 pounds to our name from a watch we sold.

We had no jobs, couldn't speak the language and didn't have a clue how we were going to survive. We just loved the weather, the beauty of the scenic area and the friendly locals we met.

Today I am still here living the Spanish dream. I have my own successful real estate business selling wonderful Spanish properties to English speaking expats from around the world embarking on their dream to live in Spain. I am also building a team of collaborating agents around the globe to help as many people as possible fulfil their dreams.

I have crossed many hurdles myself and along with past clients can share what I have learnt to help you avoid the main issues when making your move to Spain ensuring an exciting pleasurable experience for you and your family.

The first night we arrived to collect the keys from 24hr Square in Benalmadena and drove up the hill to Alhaurín El Grande. We had rented a small 1 bed cottage while our brand new 2 bed finca (country property) was being finished off. It was a stunning location with far reaching valley views and a swimming pool. Just 6 minutes from the bustling white village of Alhaurin El Grande 30 Minutes from the coast.

The first night I lay awake to the annoying buzz of a mosquito that kept bombing me, a now familiar sound. Then the dog howls started and went around the whole valley, sounds we eventually got used to.

The first morning I was up and off to the village with the kind help of my landlady to find a place for the kids in a local school. The rental agent had arranged our NIE, and I had started the residency appointment process which was a matter of visiting the National Police Station in Fuengirola with a ton of forms and photos and photocopies. With both kids now in one of the local schools it was our turn to find a job. We were the first English kids in this particular school-Salvador Gonzalez Cantos but luckily, I met a Scottish lady at the gate (later to become a best friend to this day) who also grew up in Spain and spoke the language. She advised me to go to get the Sur in English. A local paper to find local Jobs. I found a job for my husband and I and applied. It was the first ISP in Spain at the time with Americans running it and all English speaking! We were now sorted! The horses arrived 3 weeks later with paperwork in order. I then learnt that horses don't eat grass in Southern Spain and eat hay that looks like oat straw among other differences in how they are managed.

I had to drive down from the UK with the dogs once their vaccinations and papers were all up to date. A very important

Spain unlocked an expat's key to the real estate market.

lesson was to make sure the dogs had anti Leishmania collars to avoid the terrible disease, spread by mosquitos, that affects so many dogs here. Available in any pet store.

From then to now my children grew up here, had a fabulous education and outdoor lifestyle, befriending Spanish and a huge circle of expats from many different countries.

I went on to train with a large English-Speaking real estate company and stayed with them for 3 years before working with Solvia bank and then starting my own Real estate business. Which I have continued to do for the past 15 years. Recently I have Joined a rapidly growing high technology real estate company to help build cloud based professional teams of supported, self-employed agents in Spain and also globally.

I'm putting this guide together as a reference for Expats looking to move to Spain either solo, with families or with pets. I have had many experiences that I can share. Please reach out to me if you need help or advice.

- Why Spain- The Allure of the Spanish Lifestyle

The allure of the Spanish lifestyle is still today rooted in a rich blend of cultural traditions, relaxed daily rhythms, and a deep connection to family and community- something that is lacking in my home country. Here's an exploration of what makes it so captivating:

Spain unlocked an expat's key to the real estate market.

Pace of Life: Tranquilo

One of the most notable aspects of the Spanish lifestyle is the emphasis on living in the moment. In Spain, there's a saying, "No pasa nada" (don't worry about it), reflecting a general sense of calm and resilience. The siesta culture, though less prevalent in urban areas today but popular in hotter areas during the heat of the summer, symbolises this slower pace, where life is not rushed, and work-life balance is prioritised.

Cuisine and Food Culture

Food is central to Spanish life, not just as nourishment but as a social event. Long, leisurely meals with friends and family are part of daily life. Tapas, small, shared dishes, encourage socialising, while wine from regions like Rioja and Ribera del Duero is enjoyed with almost every meal. Sometimes diluted with water or fizzy water Tinto de Verano. The Mediterranean diet- based on fresh, local ingredients, in particular olive oil and a lot of fish promotes a healthy lifestyle. Some regions of Spain have the highest life expectancies in the world.

Outdoor Living and Climate

Spain's sunny climate, particularly in regions like Andalucía, Catalonia, and the Balearic Islands, encourages a healthy outdoor lifestyle. People gather in plazas, terraces, and beach promenades all year around to enjoy the sunshine. Whether it's a weekend hike in the mountains, a day at the beach, or an evening paseo (stroll), outdoor activities are definitely a part of daily life for all of us.

Spain unlocked an expat's key to the real estate market.

Sense of Community and Family

Family ties are strong in Spain, with multiple generations often living close to each other. The Spanish put a strong emphasis on communal activities, from festivals like Las Fallas or La Feria de Abril, to the shared experience of gathering at a local café or chiringuito (beach bar). Friendships and family are prioritised over individualism. Children and elderly people are welcomed in almost all situations from beach bars to late night events, there is no stigma.

Fiestas and Festivals

Spain's vibrant calendar of festivals is a testament to its lively culture. Whether it's the running of the bulls in Pamplona, La Tomatina in Buñol, or a Semana Santa's religious procession in Malaga city, Spaniards surely know how to celebrate. These events bring together locals and tourists alike, celebrating Spain's history, traditions, and joie de vivre.

Art, Music, and Culture

Spain has a long and rich cultural heritage. The works of artists like Picasso, Dalí, and Goya are globally celebrated. Flamenco, a traditional art form that originated in Andalucía, combines song, dance, and guitar to express intense emotion. Cultural appreciation is woven into daily life, from architecture (Gaudí in Barcelona) to live performances and traditional dances in all the local villages as well as nationally in big cities. In my experience Children are encouraged to dance Flamenco on stage and the elders in the village help make the traditional costumes bringing the community together.

Affordable and Quality Living

Compared to many other European countries, Spain offers a relatively affordable lifestyle especially if you move slightly away from main tourist areas. Housing, food, and transport are generally more economical, making it attractive for both expatriates and locals. Many people are drawn to the idea of enjoying a high quality of life, with access to good healthcare, education, and public services, at a reasonable cost.

Connection to Nature

From the Sierra Nevada mountains to the beaches of Costa del Sol, Spain is rich in natural beauty. This offers residents and visitors the chance to engage in a variety of outdoor activities - hiking, skiing, surfing, and more. Nature is a key part of the Spanish lifestyle, and many Spaniards make it a point to escape to the countryside, whether it's for a day trip or a holiday.

Spain unlocked an expat's key to the real estate market.

2. Understanding Spain- Climate and Weather Patterns

- Overview of Regions and Cities

Spain is a country of diverse regions, each with its own distinct identity, culture, and attractions. Here's a breakdown of some of the major regions, focusing on their unique characteristics, cultural differences, and opportunities:

Andalucía

Key Cities: Seville, Granada, Málaga, Córdoba, Cádiz

Characteristics:

Andalucía is known for its vibrant traditions, including flamenco, bullfighting and some of the most celebrated fiestas in Spain, like the Feria de Abril in Seville and Semana Santa (Holy Week).

This region is characterised by a deep Moorish influence, especially visible in its architecture, such as the stunning Alhambra in Granada and the Mezquita-Catedral in Córdoba.

The lifestyle is laid-back and reflects the Mediterranean climate, with long, warm summers and mild winters. Seaside cities like Málaga offer beachside living with a touch of history and culture.

Opportunities:

Tourism, agriculture (especially olive oil and wine), renewable energy, and real estate. With growing interest in sustainable living, Andalucía is also a hub for solar energy solutions. Sometimes to the detriment of the locals. Who are trying to protect their beautiful countryside from acres of ugly and environment destroying solar plantations.

Catalonia (Cataluña) Key Cities: Barcelona, Girona, Tarragona, Lleida

Characteristics:

Catalonia is fiercely proud of its distinct identity, language (Catalan), and cultural heritage. Barcelona, the capital, is a cosmopolitan city famous for its modernist architecture, especially the works of Antoni Gaudí, like the Sagrada Familia and Park Güell.

The region is known for its innovation and modernity, with a thriving tech scene and numerous startups. Catalonia also has a rich culinary tradition, with many Michelin-starred restaurants.

The landscape is diverse, ranging from the beaches of the Costa Brava to the Pyrenees mountains.

Opportunities:

Technology, tourism, manufacturing, and gastronomy. Barcelona, in particular, is a hub for international business and tech startups.

Madrid (Community of Madrid) the capital

Characteristics:

As Spain's capital, Madrid is a cultural and political powerhouse. The city is known for its world-class museums (Prado, Reina Sofía, Thyssen-Bornemisza), historic neighbourhoods and vibrant nightlife.

Madrid has a more continental climate, with hot summers and cold winters and it exudes a sense of grandeur with its wide boulevards, royal palaces, and grand plazas.

The people of Madrid, known as madrileños, have a reputation for being open and welcoming, with a love for socialising in the city's many bars and cafés.

Opportunities:

Finance, government, arts, media, and education. Madrid is a business hub for Spain and hosts many multinational companies' headquarters.

Valencian Community (Comunidad Valenciana) Valencia, Alicante, Castellón de la Plana

Characteristics:

Valencia is known for its modern City of Arts and Sciences, a futuristic architectural complex, and the annual Las Fallas festival, where giant paper-mâché figures are set on fire.

The region has a Mediterranean climate and is famous for its oranges and paella, the renowned Spanish dish that originated here.

The coastal city of Alicante offers beautiful beaches and a relaxed lifestyle, while the inland areas are known for their mountainous landscapes and small villages.

Opportunities:

Agriculture, tourism, and food industries. Valencia is also becoming known for its tech innovation and entrepreneurship.

Basque Country (País Vasco) Bilbao, San Sebastián, Vitoria-Gasteiz

Characteristics:

The Basque Country has a distinct culture, language (Euskara), and culinary tradition. It's renowned for its pintxos (small snacks similar to tapas) and avant-garde cuisine, with San Sebastián boasting several Michelin-starred restaurants.

Bilbao has transformed from an industrial city into a cultural hub, with the Guggenheim Museum as its centrepiece.

The region's rugged coastlines and the Pyrenees mountains make it a haven for outdoor enthusiasts, with surfing, hiking, and mountain sports being popular.

Opportunities:

Industry, technology, tourism, and gastronomy. The Basque Country has a strong economy with a focus on innovation, particularly in Bilbao.

Galicia Santiago de Compostela, A Coruña, Vigo

Characteristics:

Located in the northwest, Galicia is known for its Celtic heritage, green landscapes, and rocky coastline, including the scenic Rías Baixas fjords.

Santiago de Compostela, a UNESCO World Heritage site, is the endpoint of the famous Camino de Santiago pilgrimage route.

The region has a strong fishing industry, and seafood is central to the Galician diet. The Galicians are known for their hospitality and deep connection to their traditions.

Opportunities:

Fishing, agriculture, renewable energy, and tourism, especially tied to the Camino de Santiago.

Castile and León (Castilla y León) Valladolid, Salamanca, León, Burgos

Characteristics:

This region is steeped in history, with many medieval cities, castles, and cathedrals. Salamanca, for example, is home to one of the oldest universities in the world.

The region has a more continental climate, with harsh winters and hot summers. Its interior location gives it a more traditional feel, with a focus on agriculture and wine production.

Castile and León is famous for its robust red wines, especially those from the Ribera del Duero and Toro regions.

Opportunities:

Agriculture, wine production, and cultural tourism. Valladolid is also a political and administrative centre.

Canary Islands (Islas Canarias) Las Palmas (Gran Canaria), Santa Cruz (Tenerife)

Characteristics:

Located off the coast of northwestern Africa, the Canary Islands have a subtropical climate, making them a popular year-round destination for tourists.

Each island offers something unique: Tenerife boasts Spain's highest peak, Mount Teide; Lanzarote is known for its volcanic landscapes; and Fuerteventura offers pristine beaches.

The culture is a blend of Spanish and African influences, and the lifestyle is relaxed and centered around the outdoors.

Opportunities:

Tourism, agriculture (bananas, wine), and renewable energy. The Canary Islands are also growing as a hub for digital nomads.

Balearic Islands (Islas Baleares) Palma (Mallorca), Ibiza, Menorca

Characteristics:

The Balearic Islands are a Mediterranean paradise known for their beautiful beaches, crystal-clear waters, and vibrant nightlife, particularly on Ibiza.

Spain unlocked an expat's key to the real estate market.

Mallorca offers both luxury and tranquillity, with a mix of beautiful coastlines and quiet villages.

The islands are a prime destination for tourists, but there's also a growing focus on sustainable tourism and preserving the natural beauty of the region.

Opportunities:

Tourism, real estate, and hospitality industries are the backbone of the economy.

Spain's diverse climate regions significantly shape the country's way of life, influencing everything from daily routines and outdoor activities to housing design and energy consumption. Here's a detailed look at the various climate zones in Spain and their impact on daily life:

Mediterranean Climate (Coastal Areas: Southern and Eastern Spain)

Regions: Andalucía (Costa del Sol, Costa de la Luz), Catalonia (Costa Brava), Valencia (Costa Blanca), Balearic Islands

Characteristics:

Long, hot summers with mild winters and relatively low rainfall, particularly in the summer months. Summer temperatures regularly exceed 35°C (95°F), especially in southern Andalucía.

Winters are more temperate, making it an attractive destination for year-round outdoor activities.

Impact on Daily Life:

Outdoor Activities:

The warm, sunny climate encourages outdoor living. People spend a significant amount of time outdoors, enjoying beaches, cafés, parks, and coastal promenades. Activities like swimming, sailing, hiking, golf and tennis are popular year-round.

Housing Preferences:

Houses in Mediterranean regions are often designed with outdoor spaces such as patios, terraces, and courtyards to maximize outdoor living. Whitewashed exteriors and thick walls help keep homes cool during the hot summer months. Many older buildings lack damp proofing or insulation.

Energy Use:

Energy demand spikes in summer due to air conditioning use. However, the mild winters require less heating, making this region a good candidate for solar energy solutions. Many homes have shutters or awnings to reduce the sun's heat.

Spain unlocked an expat's key to the real estate market.

Continental Climate (Inland and Central Spain)

Regions: Madrid, Castile and León, Castile-La Mancha, Extremadura

Characteristics:

This climate features hot, dry summers and cold winters. Summer temperatures can soar above 35°C (95°F), while winters in cities like Madrid can drop below freezing, with occasional snowfall.

Rainfall is scarce, especially in the summer, contributing to the semi-arid conditions of the central plains.

Impact on Daily Life:

Outdoor Activities: In summer, outdoor activities are limited during the peak heat of the day, leading to the traditional Spanish siesta. However, mornings and late evenings are pleasant, and people often go for walks (paseo) or dine outdoors during cooler hours.

Housing Preferences:

Homes are built with insulation to handle the temperature extremes, with thicker walls and smaller windows to keep heat out in the summer and warmth in during the winter. The arid environment influences the use of water-saving landscaping techniques- like xeriscaping.

Energy Use:

Heating is essential in winter, and air conditioning is widely used in the summer. The dry, sunny conditions make the central plains ideal for solar energy development, and solar panels are becoming more common.

Oceanic Climate (Northern Spain)

Regions: Galicia, Asturias, Cantabria, Basque Country

Characteristics:

Northern Spain has a much cooler, wetter climate, influenced by the Atlantic Ocean. Rain is frequent year-round, especially in winter, and summers are mild, with temperatures ranging from 20°C to 25°C (68°F to 77°F).

Winters are mild but wet, with temperatures rarely dropping below freezing.

Impact on Daily Life:

Outdoor Activities: The cooler, greener landscape makes this region popular for outdoor activities such as hiking in the mountains, walking along rugged coastlines, and surfing on the beaches. However, the frequent rainfall means outdoor plans are often weather-dependent.

Housing Preferences:

Houses are built to handle moisture, with good drainage systems and weatherproofing to protect against constant rain. Roofs are often steep to allow water to run off easily. Wooden elements and natural stone are common in architecture.

Energy Use:

Due to the milder summers, air conditioning is less commonly needed, but heating is essential in winter. Energy consumption tends to be balanced throughout the year. This region is also investing in renewable energy, particularly wind power, due to its strong coastal winds.

Semi-Arid Climate (Southeastern Spain)

Regions:

Murcia, Almería, parts of Valencia and Alicante

Characteristics:

This is one of the driest regions in Europe, with extremely hot summers and very little rainfall. Annual rainfall can be as low as 300 mm (12 inches). Summer temperatures often exceed 35°C (95°F), while winters are mild.

Impact on Daily Life:

Outdoor Activities: The extreme summer heat limits outdoor activities during the day, with many people retreating indoors or to shaded areas. However, the coastal areas attract tourists year-round for beach activities, and water sports are popular.

Housing Preferences:

Homes are often designed to stay cool in the heat, with shaded patios, white exteriors, and tiled floors that keep interiors cool. Water conservation is essential in these areas, and rainwater collection systems are often used.

Energy Use:

High summer temperatures lead to significant air conditioning use. Due to the abundance of sunlight, this region is ideal for solar power, and many homes are equipped with solar panels.

Spain unlocked an expat's key to the real estate market.

Mountain Climate (Pyrenees, Sierra Nevada, and Cantabrian Mountains)

Regions:

Northern Spain (Pyrenees), Southern Spain (Sierra Nevada), Northwestern Spain (Cantabrian Mountains)

Characteristics:

Mountainous regions experience cooler temperatures and heavier snowfall during winter, especially in the Pyrenees and Sierra Nevada, which are popular skiing destinations. Summers are cool and dry.

Impact on Daily Life:

Outdoor Activities:

These regions are prime locations for outdoor enthusiasts. In winter, skiing and snowboarding are major attractions, while summer offers hiking, mountain biking, and climbing. Nature lovers are drawn to the stunning landscapes and wildlife.

Housing Preferences: Mountain homes are built to withstand cold winters, with steep roofs to prevent snow accumulation and heavy insulation. Fireplaces and wood-burning stoves are common features.

Energy Use:

Heating is essential during the long winters, and many homes use wood or pellet stoves for warmth. Solar energy is less common due to reduced sunlight in winter, but hydroelectric power is more prominent due to the rivers and lakes in the mountains.

Subtropical Climate (Canary Islands)

Regions: Canary Islands (Tenerife, Gran Canaria, Lanzarote, Fuerteventura)

Characteristics:

The Canary Islands have a subtropical climate, with mild temperatures year-round. Average temperatures range from 18°C (64°F) in winter to 24°C (75°F) in summer. The islands receive very little rain, especially in the southern parts.

Impact on Daily Life:

Outdoor Activities: The climate allows for year-round outdoor activities, making the islands a haven for tourists and locals alike. Beaches, water sports, and hiking are popular activities, and the islands attract visitors looking to escape colder climates.

Housing Preferences:

Homes are built to optimize outdoor living, with terraces and large windows to enjoy the views and natural light. The constant mild temperatures mean that homes don't require heavy insulation.

Energy Use:

Energy demand is stable throughout the year, with minimal heating or cooling required. The Canary Islands have significant potential for renewable energy, including wind and solar power.

Overall Impact on Energy and Housing

Energy Use Patterns:

Spain's diverse climate zones lead to varying energy demands. Coastal Mediterranean regions and central plains rely heavily on air conditioning in summer, while the northern and mountainous regions prioritize heating in winter. Solar energy is becoming more popular across the country, especially in sun-rich areas like Andalucía and Murcia.

Housing Design:

In warm climates, homes are built with features to stay cool, such as tiled floors, thick walls, and shaded patios. In colder regions, homes prioritize insulation and efficient heating systems. Climate-conscious design is increasingly focused on sustainability and energy efficiency, with renewable energy solutions like solar panels playing a key role.

- Cost of Living and Property Prices

The cost of living in Spain varies significantly depending on the region, with major urban centres like Madrid and Barcelona being notably more expensive than smaller towns, rural areas, and certain coastal regions. Here's an overview of how costs differ, focusing on property prices and the general cost of living in various areas:

Spain unlocked an expat's key to the real estate market.

Madrid: The Capital City- Cost of Living:

Madrid is one of the most expensive places to live in Spain, primarily due to its status as the capital and its strong economy. Everything from housing to entertainment is higher in cost, though public transportation is affordable.

- Property Prices:

- City Center (Salamanca, Chamberí, Retiro):

Prices for apartments in these central neighborhoods can range from €5,000 to €7,000 per square meter. Renting in the city center can cost €1,200–€2,500 per month for a modest apartment.

- Suburban Areas:

In the outskirts like Getafe or Alcobendas, prices drop to €2,500–€4,000 per square meter, making these areas more affordable, especially for families.

- Other Costs:

Dining, groceries, and services are generally more expensive in Madrid than in smaller cities, but still affordable compared to other European capitals.

Barcelona: Cosmopolitan and Costly- Cost of Living:

Like Madrid, Barcelona is one of Spain's most expensive cities. Its popularity as a cultural and business hub, combined with strong tourism, drives up living costs. However, groceries,

Spain unlocked an expat's key to the real estate market.

healthcare, and transportation remain cheaper than in many northern European cities.

- Property Prices:

- *City Center (Eixample, Gràcia, El Born):*

Prices range from €4,500 to €7,000 per square meter in central neighborhoods. Renting a one-bedroom apartment in these areas can easily cost between €1,200 and €2,000 per month.

- *Suburban Areas:*

Neighbourhoods farther from the centre, like Sants or Sant Martí, offer properties at €3,000–€4,500 per square meter, with rents around €800–€1,500 per month.

- *Other Costs:*

Public transport is affordable and dining out ranges from budget-friendly *menu del día* (set lunches) to high-end gastronomy, reflecting the city's wide range of offerings.

Andalucía: Affordable Southern Living- Cost of Living:

Andalucía is one of the most affordable regions in Spain. Daily expenses such as groceries, dining, and public services are lower here compared to Madrid and Barcelona. It's an attractive region for retirees and those seeking a more relaxed lifestyle.

- Property Prices:

  - Seville:

In the city centre, property prices range from €2,500 to €4,500 per square meter, with monthly rent for a one-bedroom apartment between €700 and €1,200. Prices drop significantly in the outskirts.

  - Málaga:

Málaga, particularly in popular areas like the historic centre, offers properties for €2,800–€5,000 per square meter. Rental prices range from €700 to €1,500 per month.

  - Countryside:

In rural areas and smaller towns like Ronda or Almería, prices can drop to €1,000–€2,500 per square meter, making it one of the most affordable regions for buying property.

  - Other Costs:

The cost of food, utilities, and transport is relatively low, with the southern lifestyle being more laid-back and economical. Solar energy, especially in Andalucía, is helping to reduce energy bills for homeowners.

Valencian Community: A Mid-Range Option- Cost of Living:

Valencia is more affordable than Madrid and Barcelona but offers a high quality of life. It's a popular destination for expatriates and those looking for a balance between urban life and beach living.

- *Property Prices:*

- Valencia City:

Property prices in the city centre, such as Ciutat Vella or Ruzafa, range from €2,500 to €4,000 per square meter. Rent for a one-bedroom apartment is typically between €800 and €1,300 per month.

- Alicante:

In Alicante, property prices range from €1,500 to €3,000 per square meter, with rents generally between €600 and €1,000 per month.

- Countryside and Smaller Towns:

Smaller towns and rural areas like Xàtiva or Gandía offer much lower prices, often between €800 and €2,000 per square meter, making property more accessible.

- Other Costs:

Valencia is known for its affordability, with low grocery costs, public transport, and an overall relaxed pace of life.

Spain unlocked an expat's key to the real estate market.

Basque Country: Higher Living Costs, Strong Economy- Cost of Living:

The Basque Country has a strong economy, high wages, and a generally higher cost of living compared to other regions, though still less expensive than Madrid or Barcelona.

- Property Prices:

- Bilbao:

Property prices in Bilbao can range from €3,500 to €5,000 per square meter in the city centre.

Renting a one-bedroom apartment typically costs €900–€1,500 per month.

- San Sebastián:

One of the most expensive cities in Spain, with property prices ranging from €4,000 to €7,500 per square meter in areas like La Concha. Rents in the city centre can easily exceed €1,200 per month.

- Smaller Towns:

Smaller towns like Vitoria-Gasteiz are more affordable, with prices ranging from €2,500 to €3,500 per square meter.

- Other Costs:

Food and services can be slightly more expensive, especially in San Sebastián, known for its high-end cuisine and Michelin-starred restaurants.

Spain unlocked an expat's key to the real estate market.

Galicia: Budget-Friendly in the Northwest - Cost of Living:

Galicia is one of Spain's most affordable regions. It offers a high quality of life at a much lower cost, especially for those seeking a more rural or quiet lifestyle. The overall cost of living, from groceries to utilities, is lower compared to other regions.

- Property Prices:

  - Santiago de Compostela:

Property prices in this historic city are relatively low, ranging from €1,500 to €3,000 per square meter. Renting a one-bedroom apartment typically costs €500–€900 per month.

  - A Coruña and Vigo:

Property prices range from €1,500 to €3,500 per square meter. Rents for one-bedroom apartments vary between €600 and €1,000 per month.

  - Countryside:

Rural areas and smaller villages offer some of the lowest property prices in Spain, ranging from €500 to €1,500 per square meter, making them an attractive option for those looking to buy affordable homes.

  - Other Costs:

Daily living costs, such as food and transport, are among the lowest in Spain. Galicia's seafood and local produce are both abundant and affordable.

Spain unlocked an expat's key to the real estate market.

Canary Islands: - Cost of Living:

The Canary Islands offer a relatively low cost of living compared to mainland Spain. Groceries, dining, and transport costs are generally affordable, though some imported goods may be more expensive due to the islands' remote location.

- Tenerife and Gran Canarian:

range from €1,800 to €3,500 per square meter in popular areas like Las Palmas or Santa Cruz. Rent for a one-bedroom apartment typically costs between €600 and €1,200 per month.

- Lanzarote and Fuerteventura:

These islands tend to be slightly more affordable, with property prices ranging from €1,500 to €3,000 per square meter, and rents generally between €500 and €1,000 per month.

- Other Costs:

The cost of utilities, such as electricity, is generally low due to the warm climate, which reduces the need for heating and cooling. Public transport is also affordable, and the overall relaxed lifestyle suits both retirees and those working remotely.

Spain unlocked an expat's key to the real estate market.

Rural Spain: Low-Cost Countryside Living

- Regions:

Extremadura, Castilla-La Mancha, Aragón, parts of Castile and León

Cost of Living

Rural areas in Spain offer some of the lowest living costs in the country. Everything from property to groceries is more affordable, and the slower pace of life allows for lower expenditures.

- Property Prices:

Extremadura:

One of the least expensive regions, with property prices as low as €600–€1,500 per square meter in small towns.

- Castilla-La Mancha:

Prices range from €800 to €2,000 per square meter, depending on proximity to major cities like Toledo.

- Other Costs:

In rural Spain, the cost of living is extremely low. However, access to services like healthcare and public transport may be more limited, and there are fewer job opportunities in some remote areas.

Spain unlocked an expat's key to the real estate market.

3. The Buying Process

- How to Start: Research and Preparation

When considering moving to Spain or purchasing property, it's essential to approach the decision with thorough research and preparation. Whether you're looking to relocate permanently, buy a second home, or invest, understanding the housing market, setting a realistic budget, and familiarizing yourself with local regulations are crucial steps. Here's an outline of key factors to consider and helpful tips:

Researching Potential Locations

- Lifestyle Preferences:

The first step is to assess your lifestyle needs and preferences. Spain offers a wide range of living environments, from bustling city centres like Madrid and Barcelona to quiet rural villages and sunny coastal towns. Consider:

- Climate:

Do you prefer a warm Mediterranean climate, a cooler northern climate, or something in between?

- Work Opportunities or Retirement:

Are you moving for work, or are you retiring and looking for a relaxed pace of life?

Spain unlocked an expat's key to the real estate market.

- Cultural Interests:

Each region has its own customs, cuisine, and way of life. Understanding these differences will help you decide which area suits you best.

- Access to Services:

Consider proximity to healthcare, schools, public transport, and other important services, especially if you're moving with a family.

- Property Market Analysis:

It's essential to research property prices and trends in the region you're considering. Spain's property market varies greatly between urban and rural areas, as well as between different regions. For example, Madrid and Barcelona have significantly higher property prices compared to rural Andalucía or Galicia.

Use online real estate platforms like Idealista, Fotocasa, Thinkspain or Kyero to compare prices in different neighbourhoods and get a sense of market trends.

Consider working with local real estate agents who can provide valuable insights into the local market and help you find hidden gems.

Understanding the Housing Market

- Urban vs. Rural:

Property in large cities such as Madrid or Barcelona tends to be more expensive but offers better access to services and amenities. In contrast, rural areas and smaller towns can provide more affordable housing but may lack the same level of infrastructure and job opportunities.

- Coastal vs. Inland:

Coastal regions, particularly along the Mediterranean and in the Balearic and Canary Islands, are more popular among tourists and expats, which can drive up property prices. Inland regions like Castilla-La Mancha or Extremadura tend to offer more affordable options.

- Rental vs. Purchase:

In some areas, it may be more practical to rent before purchasing a property, especially if you're unfamiliar with the region. Renting allows you to test the area before committing to a purchase.

- Market Trends:

Keep an eye on the market to determine if prices are rising or falling in your chosen area. Economic factors, such as Spain's tourism industry, Brexit (for UK buyers), or the local economy, can affect housing prices.

Spain unlocked an expat's key to the real estate market.

Setting a Budget

- Property Price Range:

Set a clear budget for your property purchase based on what you can afford. Keep in mind:

- Mortgage Requirements:

Non-residents can apply for Spanish mortgages, but typically banks will offer a loan of up to 60–70% of the property's value. Residents can often access mortgages of up to 80%. Ensure that your financial situation aligns with this. For advice check the link below:

https://mortgagedirectsl.com/Nicol.../Mortgage_Direct_Advice

- Additional Costs:

Purchasing property in Spain comes with additional costs. You should budget for taxes, legal fees, notary fees, and administrative costs. These can add around 10–15% to the total purchase price. Key expenses include:

- Property Transfer Tax (ITP):

6–10% of the purchase price, depending on the region.

- **Notary and Land Registry Fees:** Typically, 1–2% of the purchase price.

Spain unlocked an expat's key to the real estate market.

- Legal Fees:

A lawyer specialising in Spanish property law is essential for navigating the legal process, and their fees are typically 1–2% of the purchase price.

- Living Costs:

Consider ongoing costs such as utilities, property maintenance, local taxes, and community fees (for apartments or gated communities). If you plan to live in Spain part-time, factor in management fees if someone else will maintain the property in your absence.

- Currency Exchange Rates:

If you are buying in euros and your income or savings are in a different currency, fluctuations in exchange rates could impact your budget. Consider using a currency transfer service to lock in favourable rates. Check the link below:

https://www.lumonpay.com/referral-new/?F_ID=14365

Visiting Areas Before Making Decisions

- Firsthand Experience:

It's crucial to visit the area where you plan to buy or move. While online research can give you a good overview, nothing compares to experiencing the area firsthand. Spend time exploring the neighbourhood at different times of the day and week to understand the pace of life, traffic, noise levels, and local amenities.

- Seasonal Differences:

If you're considering coastal or rural areas, remember that these places may feel very different in summer (busy with tourists) versus winter (much quieter). Plan visits in both peak and off-peak seasons.

- Meet with Real Estate Agents:

Local real estate agents can provide a deeper understanding of the market and offer access to properties that may not be widely advertised online along with personal experiences.

- Talk to Locals:

Chatting with expats or local residents can offer valuable insights into what it's like to live in a particular area. They can share their experiences with local services, weather conditions, or community life. There are many groups on social media such as facebook where you can ask locals questions.

https://www.facebook.com/groups/propertyinspaingroup

https://www.facebook.com/groups/movetocostadelsolspain

Starting the Legal and Financial Process Early

- Hire a Lawyer:

It's strongly recommended to hire an independent lawyer who specialises in Spanish property law. They can:

- Help you understand local laws and regulations.

- Check that the property has a clear title and is free of debts.

Spain unlocked an expat's key to the real estate market.

- Ensure that planning permissions and building regulations are up to code.

- NIE (Foreigner's Identification Number):

As a non-resident, you'll need to obtain an NIE number to buy property or open a bank account in Spain. Start the process early, as it can take several weeks to secure.

To obtain an NIE (Número de Identificación de Extranjero) in Spain, you can download the required forms online from the official Spanish government websites. Here's how you can access the forms and additional details:

Form EX-15 (Application for NIE)

- Where to Download:

You can download the NIE application form (EX-15) directly from the Spanish Ministry of the Interior's website.

- Link to Form EX-15 (PDF):

EX-15Form

https://extranjeros.inclusion.gob.es/es/ModelosSolicitudes/Mod_solicitudes2/15-Formulario_solicitud_NIE_y_certificados.pdf

- Filling Out the Form:

This form must be filled out in Spanish. You'll need to provide your personal details, explain why you need the NIE, and give information about where you'll be staying in Spain.

Spain unlocked an expat's key to the real estate market.

Form 790 (Tax Payment for NIE Application)

- Where to Download:

You'll also need Form 790, which is used to pay the corresponding fee for the NIE application (around €10-12, depending on the region).

- Link to Form 790 (PDF):

Form 790 (Code 012)]

https://sede.policia.gob.es/Tasa790_012/

- Filling Out the Form:

This form allows you to pay the required tax at a local bank. After filling it out online, you can print it, pay at a bank, and bring the receipt along with the EX-15 form to your NIE appointment.

Where to Submit Your Application

- At a Spanish Police Station or Foreigners' Office:

You must submit these forms in person at a police station or foreigners' office (Oficina de Extranjería) in Spain, or at a Spanish consulate abroad if applying from another country.

- Appointment (Cita Previa):

Most places will require you to book an appointment in advance (cita previa). You can do this on the official website for immigration appointments:

Cita Previa for NIE

Spain unlocked an expat's key to the real estate market.

https://sede.administracionespublicas.gob.es/icpplus/index.html

Required Documents

- Completed EX-15 form

- Form 790 and proof of payment

- Valid passport and a photocopy

- Passport-sized photographs (some offices may request this)

- A written explanation (in Spanish) for why you need the NIE (e.g., property purchase, business, employment, etc.)

By downloading these forms and preparing the necessary documentation in advance, you can streamline the NIE application process. The cost of hiring a lawyer to assist with the NIE application process in Spain varies depending on the lawyer, their location, and the complexity of your situation. Typically, legal fees for NIE assistance range between €100 and €300.

- Open a Spanish Bank Account:

To facilitate the financial aspects of buying a property, including mortgage payments and utility bills, you will need to open a bank account in Spain. Choose a bank that offers good services for international clients. It is now possible to have an online bank with a Spanish IBAN number such as Revolut and N26. Both Revolut and N26 are digital banks that operate across Europe, including Spain. They offer a fully online banking experience, making them popular among expats, travellers, and tech-savvy individuals. You can sign up here:

https://revolut.com/referral/?referral-code=nicolabuwp!DEC1-24-VR-ES

Negotiating and Making an Offer

- Property Surveys:

In some cases, It's a good idea to have a property survey carried out to ensure there are no structural issues or hidden problems. In some cases, surveys are not required, but they offer peace of mind, especially for older properties.

- Negotiation:

Don't be afraid to negotiate the asking price. Having a clear understanding of the market will help you make a competitive offer. Be aware that a lot of Spanish vendors will not accept offers.

- Reservation Agreement:

Once your offer is accepted, you'll typically sign a reservation agreement and pay a deposit (usually 3000 to 10,000 euros) to your own lawyer into a client account. This removes the property from the market while your lawyer conducts due diligence.

Final Steps: Closing the Sale

- Private Purchase Contract:

Once the legal checks are complete, a private purchase contract is signed. At this stage, you'll pay an additional deposit (often 10% of the property price). Usually about 2 weeks after the reservation is paid.

- Completion:

On the agreed completion date, the final payment is made, and the sale is completed at the notary's office. You'll sign the deed of sale (escritura), and the property will be transferred to your name. Typically, about 4 weeks after the 10% private purchase contract. Although a mortgage application will take 6 weeks.

Key Tips:

- Start Early:

Research locations, understand the housing market, get legal advice early in the process, get your mortgage pre-approved before you start your search and by getting your currency exchange company set up before the search can save you time, money, and stress.

- Take Your Time:

Don't rush into a decision. Visit potential areas, evaluate different properties, and gather as much information as possible before committing.

Spain unlocked an expat's key to the real estate market.

- *Consult Experts:*

Legal advice, financial advice, and local knowledge are invaluable when purchasing property abroad. Partner with trusted professionals to guide you through the process.

- Choosing the Right Location for Your Lifestyle

Match different regions or cities with varying expat needs. For example, retirees might prefer quieter coastal towns, while young professionals might enjoy the vibrant cities.

- Understanding the Buying Process: Steps and Timeline

Here's a step-by-step guide to buying property in Spain, from the initial search to closing the deal. The timeline will vary, but on average, expect a process lasting about 2 to 4 months.

Step 1: Initial Search (1-3 weeks)

Start by identifying the type of property you want and the region, whether it's coastal, urban, or rural. Browse online property portals and consider enlisting a real estate agent specialising in your desired area, which can save time and ensure legal clarity.

Step 2: Property Viewing & Selection (1-4 weeks)

Once you've shortlisted properties, schedule viewings. If you're an expat, it's especially helpful to have an agent who can guide you through neighbourhoods, legal requirements, and local considerations.

Step 3: Make an Offer and Reserve the Property (1-2 weeks)

When you're ready to make an offer, negotiate through your agent. Once an offer is accepted, sign a "reserva" contract (reservation contract) and pay a small deposit to your lawyer held in a client account (around €3,000 to €10,000). This holds the property and takes it off the market.

Step 4: Legal Representation and Due Diligence (2-3 weeks)

Instruct a Spanish lawyer to perform due diligence on the property, ensuring there are no debts, legal issues, or encumbrances. Your lawyer will also guide you through acquiring an NIE (foreigners' identification number) and setting up a Spanish bank account if needed.

Step 5: Sign the Preliminary Contract and Pay a Deposit (1-2 weeks)

Once due diligence is complete, sign a private purchase contract (Contrato de Arras) and pay a deposit (usually 10% of the purchase price). This contract legally binds both buyer and seller.

Step 6: Obtain Financing, if Necessary (4-6 weeks)

If you're applying for a mortgage, now's the time to finalise it with a bank. Spanish banks often take up to 6 weeks to process mortgages, including property valuation and document checks.

Step 7: Finalise the Purchase and Sign at the Notary (1 week)

The last step is to meet at a notary office to sign the property deed (Escritura de Compraventa) and pay the remaining balance. Both buyer and seller need to be present, along with your lawyer and a notary. The notary registers the sale with the property registry.

Step 8: Post-Sale Registration and Taxes (1-2 weeks)

After the notary visit, your lawyer will register the deed and pay associated taxes, like Transfer Tax (ITP) or VAT, and Notary fees. You'll also update utilities and community charges in your name.

- Key Considerations: New Builds vs. Resales

When comparing new-build homes and resale properties in Spain, several factors specific to the Spanish real estate market play a key role. These include the quality of construction, completion timelines, taxation, and potential resale value, all of which are shaped by Spanish property laws and buyer preferences.

Quality

New-Build Homes:

Pros:

Modern construction standards: New-build homes in Spain must adhere to strict EU regulations regarding energy efficiency and safety (e.g., thermal insulation and renewable energy integration, such as solar panels). This can lead to lower utility bills.

Customization:

Many Spanish developers allow buyers to personalize finishes (tiles, kitchen fittings, etc.), particularly if buying off-plan.

Warranty:

By law, new-build properties in Spain come with a 10-year structural guarantee (Seguro Decenal), which covers significant defects. This is a major advantage in case of unforeseen issues.

Cons:

Varying quality: Not all developers deliver the same quality. In Spain, some mass developments may prioritize speed over workmanship, leading to issues like poor soundproofing or less durable materials.

Settling issues: Like anywhere, new properties in Spain can experience settling, which may result in cracks in the first few years.

Resale Properties:

Pros:

Proven durability: Older properties, especially those built before the construction boom of the early 2000s, tend to be more robust. In places like Andalucía or Madrid, many traditional houses are known for their solid build quality.

Character:

Resale homes in Spain, particularly those in older towns or rural areas, often feature charming characteristics like stone walls, terracotta floors, or wooden beams, which are highly valued.

Spain unlocked an expat's key to the real estate market.

Cons:

Potential renovations: Older homes might need updates, such as new plumbing, electrical wiring, or insulation, especially in historic areas where preservation limits can affect upgrades.

Energy efficiency:

Pre-2000 homes are typically less energy-efficient, potentially resulting in higher running costs compared to modern builds.

Timeline for Completion

New-Build Homes:

Pros:

Future planning: New-build projects in Spain often allow buyers to lock in a price and plan financially while the home is under construction. This can be beneficial for buyers who are in no rush to move.

Cons:

Delays: As in many countries, construction delays are common in Spain, particularly due to issues like contractor shortages or legal paperwork related to obtaining building permits. This is especially common in areas where demand for new properties is high, such as along the Costa del Sol.

Ongoing construction:

If you're buying in a large development, parts of the community may still be under construction after you move in, impacting your comfort.

Resale Properties:

Pros:

Immediate availability:

Once the sale is completed (which can take 2–3 months depending on mortgage approval and legal checks), you can move in right away, which is ideal for those who want to relocate quickly.

Cons:

Unpredictable negotiation time:

While generally faster than waiting for a new-build, negotiation processes can still stretch out, especially in competitive markets like Barcelona or Marbella.

Taxation Differences

New-Build Homes:

Pros:

Lower VAT (IVA):

In Spain, new-build properties are subject to 10% VAT (IVA) on the purchase price, plus an additional 1.5% Stamp Duty (AJD), which is lower than the tax on resale properties.

Possible incentives:

There are occasionally government incentives, such as lower mortgage rates for first-time buyers or subsidies for energy-efficient homes, particularly for sustainable builds in regions promoting green energy.

Cons:

Additional costs: New builds can come with additional administrative costs, like developer fees, notary fees, and registration costs, which need to be factored into your budget.

Resale Properties:

Pros:

Lower initial price but higher taxes:

While resale homes can be cheaper, the taxes are generally higher. Resale properties in Spain are subject to the Transfer Tax (Impuesto de Transmisiones Patrimoniales, ITP), which varies by region and ranges from 6% to 10% of the purchase price, depending on the region (e.g., 10% in Andalucía, 6% in Madrid for properties under a certain value).

Cons:

No VAT:

Resale properties don't have VAT but come with the higher ITP, which might increase the overall upfront cost of the purchase compared to a new build, especially in regions with higher rates.

Resale Value

New-Build Homes:

Pros:

Modern appeal:

New-build homes in Spain, particularly in desirable locations like the Costa Brava or Costa del Sol, may appeal to future buyers due to their energy efficiency and modern features, such as smart home technology.

Fewer repairs:

With a new home, future buyers are less likely to worry about repairs, which can be a selling point.

Cons:

Depreciation:

In Spain, new-build homes are often sold at a premium, and this can result in an initial depreciation in value once you move in. As the property ages, its "new" status fades, and the price may stabilize or even drop initially.

Overdevelopment risk:

In some popular regions, there's a risk of overdevelopment, particularly in coastal areas like Murcia or Alicante. An oversupply of similar new homes can suppress resale prices.

Resale Properties:

Pros:

Established areas:

Older homes are often located in mature, desirable neighbourhoods with established infrastructure, like good schools, transport, and services, which hold their value better.

Character-driven demand:

In historic cities like Seville or Granada, unique architectural features and charm make older homes highly sought after, which can positively impact resale value.

Spain unlocked an expat's key to the real estate market.

Cons:

Renovation costs: To attract buyers, you might need to invest in modernizing or refurbishing, especially in older or less energy-efficient properties.

Both options can be good investments depending on the location— coastal areas like the Costa del Sol, urban centres like Madrid or Barcelona, or historic cities like Seville each have their own dynamics that affect property prices and demand.

Financial Aspects

- Buying Costs: What to Expect

When buying a property in Spain, it's essential to account for a variety of additional costs beyond the property's purchase price. These extra fees typically range from 10% to 15% of the property's total value. Below is a detailed breakdown of these costs, including notary fees, registration costs, survey fees, and other potential expenses.

Property Transfer Taxes

The most significant cost after the property price is the applicable taxes, which vary depending on whether you're buying a new-build or a resale property.

New-Build Properties:

- VAT (IVA): 10% of the purchase price for residential properties. For public housing (VPO), the rate is 4%

- *Stamp Duty (Actos Jurídicos Documentados, AJD):*

Varies by region, typically between 0.5% and 1.5% of the property price. For example, it's 1.5% in Andalucía.

Resale Properties:

- Transfer Tax (Impuesto de Transmisiones Patrimoniales, ITP):

Varies by region, typically between 6% and 10% Examples include:

  - 10% in regions like Cataluña

  - 7% in Andalucía.

  - 6-8% in Madrid, depending on property value.

  - 7% in the Canary Islands.

Notary Fees (Notaría)

These fees are set by law and are based on the property's value, but they generally range between €600 and €1,200. The notary is responsible for preparing the sale deed (Escritura Pública) and witnessing its signing.

- Expect to pay around 0.5% of the property's price in notary fees.

Land Registry Fees (Registro de la Propiedad)

The property must be registered at the Land Registry, and these fees are also based on the value of the property. They typically range from €400 to €1,000.

- 0.2% to 0.5% of the property price is a common estimate for this cost.

Legal Fees (Abogado)

It is highly advisable to hire a lawyer to guide you through the property purchase process in Spain. Legal fees usually range from 1% to 1.5% of the property's value, depending on the complexity of the transaction.

- €1,000 to €3,000 is typical for most transactions, but higher fees can apply for high-value properties or more intricate cases.

Survey Fees (Tasación)

While not mandatory, it is highly recommended to have an independent survey (tasación) done to assess the property's condition and market value. If you are applying for a mortgage, a survey is usually required by the bank.

- Costs for a surveyor range from €300 to €600 depending on the size and location of the property.

Mortgage-Related Costs

If you are using a mortgage to purchase the property, several additional costs will arise:

- *Valuation Fee (Tasación):*
This is required by the bank to assess the value of the property. It typically costs between €300 and €600, depending on the property size and location.

- *Mortgage Notary Fees:*
If you are taking out a mortgage, there will be additional notary fees for the mortgage deed. These can range from €500 to €1,000.

- Mortgage Registry Fee:

Similar to property registration, the mortgage needs to be registered with the Land Registry, costing between €200 and €400

- Bank Arrangement Fees (Comisión de Apertura):

Many banks charge a fee for setting up the mortgage, often 1% to 1.5% of the mortgage loan amount.

Banking Costs

When transferring money for the purchase, there may be international bank transfer fees and currency exchange costs if you're buying from abroad. These vary depending on the bank and exchange service used.

- Bank transfer fees may range from €30 to €300, depending on the bank and the amount transferred. Using a Currency exchange company can sometimes eliminate this.

- *Currency exchange fees:*

If purchasing from outside the Eurozone, using a currency exchange broker will minimize costs as banks usually charge a margin of 1% to 3%.

Estate Agent Fees (Agente Inmobiliario)

In Spain, the estate agent's commission is generally paid by the seller, not the buyer. However, it's important to be aware that the commission paid by the seller is typically 3% to 5% of the sale price.

- Buyer fees:

In some cases, an estate agent might charge the buyer a fee (e.g., for extra services or specific market assistance)

Home Insurance

Home insurance is not legally required for property purchases, but it is mandatory if you are taking out a mortgage. Basic home insurance typically costs between €150 and €300 annually, but more comprehensive coverage will be higher.

Utility Connection Fees

For new-build properties, you may also need to pay for the installation or connection of utilities such as water, electricity, and gas.

- Utility connection fees can range from €200 to €500 depending on the provider and services required.

Other Administrative Costs

- NIE Number: If you are a non-Spanish resident buying property, you will need an NIE (Número de Identificación de Extranjero). This is necessary for property purchases and can be obtained through Spanish embassies or local authorities.

 - The fee for obtaining an NIE is usually around €10 to €20, but some legal advisors charge an extra fee for managing the application, which can range from €50 to €200.

Spain unlocked an expat's key to the real estate market.

Maintenance Fees (Community Fees)

If you are buying an apartment or a property within a community (urbanización), there will be regular community maintenance fees to cover shared areas (pools, gardens, security, etc.). These vary greatly based on location, services, and property type.

- Monthly community fees typically range from €60 to €250 but can be higher for luxury developments.

Total Additional Costs Estimate:

For a new-build or resale property in Spain, expect additional costs to add up to around 10% to 15% of the property price, including taxes, legal fees, and other associated costs. Being aware of these costs upfront can help avoid any surprises during the purchase process.

What are "AFO," "DAFO," and "SAFO" certifications?

They are certificates related to the legal and regulatory compliance of rural properties, especially in areas where informal or unregulated buildings have been common. These certifications help buyers, sellers, and authorities assess a property's legal standing and suitability for purchase.

AFO/DAFO Certificate Cost

The cost typically ranges from €1,500 to €3,000, though it can be higher if the property is particularly large or complex. This includes municipal fees, inspections, technical reports, and possibly legal advice if there are any outstanding compliance issues.

To apply for an AFO, a qualified architect or surveyor must conduct a thorough inspection of the property. Hiring an independent architect could add €500 to €1,000 depending on the property's condition and size.

There may be additional legal fees, which typically range from €500 to €1,500

SAFO (like AFO) processes generally have similar cost structures but may vary slightly by region or property. Because the exact requirements and fees vary widely across municipalities in Spain, it's wise to consult with local authorities or real estate professionals to get an accurate estimate.

AFO (Asimilado Fuera de Ordenación)

   - The AFO (Asimilado Fuera de Ordenación) is a legal status for buildings in non-urban (typically rural) areas that were constructed without the proper licenses but have existed for a certain time and are no longer subject to enforcement action. It essentially gives the building a "semi-legal" status, allowing for basic maintenance but prohibiting expansions.

   - An AFO does not make the property fully compliant with current building codes, but it allows the building to be connected to essential services (like electricity and water) and makes it easier for buyers to obtain financing.

DAFO (Declaración de Asimilado Fuera de Ordenación)

- DAFO is the official declaration process through which a property obtains the AFO status. The property owner or seller must apply for the DAFO to obtain an AFO certificate, which formally registers the property as an "assimilated out of regulation."

- This certificate can reassure buyers, as it ensures that the property is recognized by local authorities and meets certain standards, even if it does not have full planning approval.

SAFO (Situación Asimilado Fuera de Ordenación)

- The SAFO (Situación Asimilado Fuera de Ordenación) is similar to the AFO but may refer to buildings that have been "out of order" for a longer period or in specific contexts.

- Like the AFO, the SAFO acknowledges that the building does not have all the permits or planning permissions of new construction but has been in place long enough to be immune to legal action.

These certifications play a crucial role in rural property transactions, especially in Andalusia, by helping to clarify property rights and potential risks for buyers and by making older, informal buildings more marketable.

Building on rustic (rural) land in Spain is generally more restricted than on urban land due to regulations designed to preserve agricultural areas, natural landscapes, and environmental resources. However, under certain conditions, construction on rustic land can be allowed. Here's what to know:

Building on Rustic land

Types of Rustic Land and Zoning Restriction

- Rustic land can be classified differently depending on local regulations, with categories like protected, non-developable, or developable with limitations.

- Protected rustic land, which includes natural reserves, forest areas, or agricultural land, has the strictest restrictions, often prohibiting construction entirely or only allowing specific structures like agricultural buildings.

Permitted Structures on Rustic Land

- Agricultural Use: Generally, construction is limited to agricultural use, such as farmhouses, barns, or buildings that support rural economic activities like livestock or forestry.

- Residential Use: Building a residential home is usually restricted but can be possible under certain criteria. For instance, in some regions, owners can build a residence if the land parcel is large enough, typically a minimum of 10,000 to 25,000 square meters in Andalucia.

- Tourism and Leisure: Some regions may allow cnstruction for rural tourism or eco-tourism businesses, such as small hotels, hostels, or rental cottages, with strict guidelines on environmental impact.

Applying for a Building Permit

- Licenses and Permits: To build on rustic land, you must obtain a Licencia Urbanística (urban planning license) from the local town hall. In most cases, it's advisable to consult with an architect or legal advisor to ensure the project aligns with local zoning laws.

- DAFO/AFO Certification: If you're looking to purchase or renovate an existing building on rustic land, applying for a DAFO or AFO (as previously explained) can be necessary to legalize structures that were built without prior approval.

Compliance with Building Standards

- Buildings on rustic land must comply with regional building standards, including environmental and aesthetic requirements that aim to integrate structures into the natural landscape.

- New homes may need to be eco-friendly or low-impact, particularly in areas that prioritize environmental conservation.

Alternative Building Options

- For some types of rural land, temporary or semi-permanent structures like prefabricated homes or eco-friendly tiny homes can be an alternative, though they still require municipal approval and adherence to local land-use laws.

- Small agricultural facilities, warehouses, or other non-residential structures may be allowed more easily than full residential buildings.

Penalties for Unauthorised Construction

- Building without the required licenses on rustic land can lead to fines, demolition orders, or inability to connect to essential services like water and electricity.

Since regulations differ across regions (e.g., Andalusia, Valencia, Catalonia), it's wise to work with a local expert in Spanish property law to ensure any building project is legal and feasible.

- Mortgages: Options and Requirements

Mortgages for expats in Spain are widely available, but the process can differ somewhat from what local's experience. Banks may have stricter requirements for non-residents, and down payments can be higher. Here's an overview of how mortgages work for expats in Spain, including documentation, down payment requirements, and the differences between fixed and variable interest rates.

Types of Mortgages for Expats

Expats can generally access the same types of mortgages as Spanish residents, but with different conditions. These include:

- Resident Mortgages:

Available if you live and pay taxes in Spain. These typically come with better terms, like lower interest rates and higher loan-to-value (LTV) ratios.

- Non-Resident Mortgages:

For those who don't reside in Spain full-time. These often require a higher down payment and may have slightly higher interest rates.

Down Payment Requirements

- Non-residents:

For non-residents, Spanish banks usually offer a maximum of 60-70% of the property's value (loan-to-value, or LTV). This means you'll need to cover 30-40% as a down payment.

- Residents:

If you are a resident in Spain, banks are typically more flexible, offering up to 80% LTV of the property's value, meaning you'll need a down payment of around 20%.

In addition to the down payment, you will need to budget for the closing costs (taxes, notary, legal fees), which are usually 10-15%

The 90 days in 180 rule

Countries Affected by the 90/180 Rule:

All non-EU, non-Schengen countries whose citizens can enter the Schengen Area without a visa for short stays:

United States

Canada

Australia

Spain unlocked an expat's key to the real estate market.

New Zealand

Japan

South Korea

Brazil

Argentina

Israel

United Kingdom (post-Brexit)

And many others with visa-waiver agreements for short stays.

The Rule:

- Non EU and non-Schengen countries citizens can stay in the Schengen Area (which includes Spain and most other EU countries) for up to 90 days within any 180-day period without a visa.

- This 90-day limit applies to tourist visits, business trips, or family visits, but it doesn't apply if you have a visa or residency permit for longer stays.

How the 180-Day Period Works:

- The 180-day period is rolling, meaning it is always calculated backward from the current date.

- You need to count back 180 days from the date you want to enter a Schengen country and ensure that you haven't already spent 90 days within that period.

Spain unlocked an expat's key to the real estate market.

How It Impacts Travel:

- If you spend a full 90 days in the Schengen Zone, you'll have to leave and wait 90 days before re-entering.

- Shorter visits are cumulative. For example, if you stay for 30 days in Spain, leave for 60 days, and then return, you'll have 60 days remaining in your current 180-day window.

Consequences of Overstaying:

- Overstaying the 90-day limit can lead to fines, deportation, or even bans on re-entry to the Schengen Area.

For those spending more time in Spain, alternatives like long-stay visas or residency permits (such as the non-lucrative visa or Golden Visa) may be needed.

Wills in Spain

Why I need a will

Having a Spanish will is essential if you own property or other assets in Spain, and here are the main reasons why:

1. Simplifies the Process for Heirs: A Spanish will streamlines the inheritance process in Spain, ensuring that your estate is divided according to your wishes with minimal delays and complications. Without it, the process can become complex, especially if your foreign will needs to be validated in Spain.

2. Avoids Conflicts Between Wills: If you already have a will in another country, a Spanish will can be set up specifically to

handle your assets in Spain, avoiding any potential conflicts between different legal systems.

3. Reduces Time and Costs: Without a Spanish will, the probate process can be lengthy and costly as it involves verifying foreign documents and translating them into Spanish, which can add both time and expense.

4. Tax Benefits: Spanish inheritance tax laws vary significantly, and having a Spanish will can help you plan more efficiently, potentially reducing the inheritance tax liability for your heirs.

5. Clearer Distribution of Assets: Spanish law allows non-residents to apply the inheritance laws of their nationality to their Spanish assets. However, without a Spanish will, Spanish law may default to its own succession laws, which may distribute assets differently than you intended.

Visas: Types and How to Obtain Them

Non-Lucrative Visa

Purpose:

Designed for individuals who want to live in Spain (or other countries offering this option) without engaging in any professional activity or employment within the country.

Key Requirements:

Financial proof:

You must demonstrate you have sufficient financial means to support yourself. In Spain, this is typically 400% of the IPREM

(Indicador Público de Renta de Efectos Múltiples), which amounts to around €28,000 per year (higher if bringing family).

Private health insurance:

You must have private health insurance valid in Spain.

No criminal record.

No employment:

You cannot work while in the country, but you can manage your investments remotely (i.e., digital nomads could qualify as long as their income isn't tied to Spanish companies).

Validity:

Usually issued for one year, renewable for two-year periods, with eligibility for long-term residency after five years.

Golden Visa (Investor Visa)

Purpose: Aimed at attracting wealthy individuals who are willing to make a significant investment in the country, typically in real estate, businesses, or government bonds.

Key Requirements:

Property investment: In Spain, the minimum real estate investment is €500,000.

Other investments:

Alternatively, you can invest €2 million in Spanish government bonds, €1 million in shares or bank deposits, or start a business that generates jobs and local economic activity.

Health insurance and no criminal record.

Spain unlocked an expat's key to the real estate market.

Work authorization:

Unlike the non-lucrative visa, golden visa holders can work and live in the country.

No residency requirement:

You are not required to live in the country for a minimum period, making it ideal for those who want flexibility.

Validity:

Initially valid for two years, renewable every five years. After five years, you can apply for permanent residency.

Work Visa/Permit

Purpose:

For individuals who intend to work and live in the country legally.

Types:

Employee Visa (for salaried workers): Requires a job offer from a company in the country, which must first prove that no suitable local candidates are available for the role.

Self-employed Visa:

For individuals who wish to set up their own business or work as freelancers.

Spain unlocked an expat's key to the real estate market.

Key Requirements:

Job offer:

For an employee visa, the employer must initiate the application process and provide proof of your qualifications and the need for a foreign worker.

Proof of qualifications:

For skilled positions, you may need to prove your education or relevant experience.

Health insurance and no criminal record.

Validity:

Typically tied to the length of the employment contract or business plan, renewable annually or biannually.

Entrepreneur Visa

Purpose:

For entrepreneurs who plan to start an innovative business in the country.

Key Requirements:

Business plan: Your business must demonstrate innovation and potential for job creation.

Sufficient capital:

You need to show that you have the financial means to support the venture.

Validity:

Initially for one year, renewable as long as the business is operational.

Student Visa

Purpose:

For individuals planning to study in the country.

Key Requirements:

Acceptance into a recognized educational institution.

Proof of financial resources to cover living costs during the study period.

Health insurance.

Work rights:

In Spain, students can work up to 20 hours per week.

Family Reunification Visa

Purpose:

For family members of a legal resident or citizen of the country.

Key Requirements:

Proof of family relationship (spouse, children, or dependent parents).

The sponsor must have sufficient financial means to support the family.

Health insurance.

Spain unlocked an expat's key to the real estate market.

Digital Nomad Visa (in progress or recently introduced in some countries, like Spain)

Purpose:

Tailored for remote workers or freelancers whose income comes from non-local sources.

Key Requirements:

Proof of remote work:

You need to demonstrate that your income is derived from companies or clients outside of the country.

Minimum income threshold:

Must meet a minimum monthly income requirement (still being finalized in some countries).

Health insurance.

Validity:

Likely to be granted for 1 year with the option of renewal.

Working with Professionals

- Finding the Right Real Estate Agent

When choosing a trustworthy real estate agent, especially as an expat, it's crucial to ensure they have the knowledge, experience, and communication skills to meet your needs. Here's how to select a reliable real estate agent:

Spain unlocked an expat's key to the real estate market.

Local Knowledge and Expertise

- *Why it matters:*

A good agent should be deeply familiar with the area you're interested in, including property values, local regulations, taxes, and the overall market trends. They should also be aware of neighbourhoods that meet your specific requirements (e.g., schools, transport links, or amenities).

- *How to check:*

Ask about their recent transactions in the area, how long they've been working locally, and if they specialize in certain types of properties (e.g., luxury, vacation homes, investment properties).

Language Proficiency and Communication

- *Why it matters:*

Especially for expats, language barriers can complicate the home-buying process. Look for an agent fluent in your language, as this will ensure smooth communication and avoid misunderstandings during negotiations, contract signings, and discussions about complex local regulations.

- *How to check:*

Speak with the agent directly and assess their fluency and ease in communicating important details in your preferred language. You may also ask if they've worked with expat clients before.

Credentials and Licensing

- *Why it matters:*

A legitimate real estate agent will have the proper certifications, licenses, and affiliations with recognized professional bodies. In Spain, for instance, real estate agents should ideally be affiliated with API (Agente de la Propiedad Inmobiliaria) or GIPE (Gestor Intermediario en Promociones de Edificaciones), indicating they've met professional standards.

- *How to check:*

Ask to see their credentials and verify their registration with local regulatory bodies. You can also search for reviews or feedback online from previous clients.

Track Record and Reputation

- *Why it matters:*

A trustworthy agent will have a solid reputation for delivering results and providing excellent customer service.

- *How to check:*

Look for reviews and testimonials on their website, Google, or other real estate platforms. You may also ask for references from previous clients or search for any complaints filed against them.

Professional Network

- *Why it matters:*

A well-connected agent can introduce you to essential contacts, such as mortgage brokers, notaries, and lawyers, making the buying process smoother.

- How to check:

Ask about their relationships with local professionals and whether they can provide recommendations or offer a more comprehensive service.

Commitment to Transparency

- Why it matters:

A trustworthy agent will be transparent about fees, commissions, and the overall process. Be wary of agents who are unclear about these details or who pressure you into decisions.

- How to check:

Have an initial conversation about their fee structure and whether it aligns with your expectations. Ensure they provide you with all the necessary information upfront.

Using MLS and Property Portals for Property Searches

In your search for property, leveraging Multiple Listing Services (MLS) and property portals can provide a significant advantage. Here's how to use them effectively:

Multiple Listing Services (MLS)

- What is MLS?:

MLS is a database that allows real estate brokers to share property listings with each other, ensuring that buyers have access to a wide range of properties on the market. MLS systems are particularly popular in many countries, including Spain.

- Why it's useful:

With MLS, your real estate agent can access a wide variety of listings, making it easier to find the type of property you want. It also fosters transparency since agents share property information, reducing the risk of missing out on good opportunities. In theory you only need to work with one agent and they can arrange all the viewings with all the other agents saving you time and effort. Giving you access to all available properties.

Property Portals

- Popular portals in Spain

- Idealista.com

One of Spain's largest property portals, listing homes for sale and rent across the country. You can filter properties by price, location, and more.

- Fotocasa.es

Another major property search engine that lists residential properties, holiday homes, and even new builds.

- Rightmove (Overseas):

useful for expats, Rightmove lists properties available for sale in Spain, allowing you to browse in English.

- Kyero.com

Focused on foreign buyers looking for homes in Spain, Kyero lists properties in different regions, including English-language descriptions.

- *Why they're useful:*

Property portals allow you to conduct independent research and browse available listings before reaching out to an agent. This empowers you to make informed decisions and provides a clearer idea of market pricing. Some portals also offer resources for expats, like guides on buying property in foreign countries and legal requirements.

Tips for Using MLS and Property Portals

Property portals are not always up to date and sometimes have false properties. The best way to work with portals is to send the links you like to your chosen agent and they will check out the property for you.

- *Set filters:*

Use price, location, and property type filters to narrow your search. This will save you time by showing properties that meet your criteria.

- *Compare properties:*

Use the information from portals to compare similar listings. This will help you gauge whether a property is priced fairly.

- *Stay updated:*

Many portals offer notification services when new properties matching your criteria become available.

- *Cross-check listings:*

Listings may appear on multiple platforms, so cross-checking them will help you see whether agents are marketing a property consistently across various portals.

By combining a trustworthy agent with these powerful search tools, you can streamline your property search, making it easier to find the right home while avoiding common pitfalls.

- Engaging a Lawyer: Why It's Essential

When buying property in Spain, hiring a Spanish lawyer (abogado) who specialises in property law is one of the most important steps to protect your investment and ensure the process goes smoothly. Here's why it's crucial:

Ensuring Compliance with Spanish Property Law

- *Why it matters:*

Spanish property law can be complex and significantly different from other countries' legal systems. Local regulations, taxes, and land ownership laws need to be followed precisely to avoid legal issues. A specialised property lawyer will ensure that the entire transaction complies with Spanish law, safeguarding you from future disputes or legal challenges.

- *What the lawyer does:*

They will review the sales contract, verify property ownership, and confirm that the property is free of encumbrances (such as debts, liens, or legal claims). They will also ensure that all necessary permits and licenses are in place.

Title and Ownership Verification

- Why it matters:

In Spain, it's essential to confirm the legal ownership of a property before purchase. In some cases, the seller may not have clear title to the property, or there may be restrictions or disputes tied to it.

- What the lawyer does:

They will perform due diligence, checking the Land Registry (Registro de la Propiedad) to verify that the seller has clear title and that there are no outstanding debts or mortgages on the property. This process ensures you will own the property outright without facing claims from third parties.

Protecting Your Deposit

- Why it matters:

In Spain, it is common to pay a deposit (typically 10% of the property's value) when signing a private purchase contract (contrato de arras). If something goes wrong, such as the seller backing out of the deal, your deposit might be at risk. Your lawyer will help protect you.

- What the lawyer does:

They will draft or review the private purchase contract to include protective clauses that allow you to recover your deposit if the seller violates the agreement. This prevents potential financial loss due to disputes or contract irregularities.

Spain unlocked an expat's key to the real estate market.

Managing Taxes and Fees

- Why it matters:

Property transactions in Spain come with various taxes and fees, such as the Property Transfer Tax (Impuesto sobre Transmisiones Patrimoniales - ITP) or VAT (IVA) for new properties, as well as Notary and Land Registry fees. Miscalculating these can result in unexpected costs.

- What the lawyer does:

They will provide an accurate breakdown of all applicable taxes and fees so that you can plan your budget accordingly. They also ensure that the tax payments are made on time to avoid fines or penalties.

Handling the Closing Process

- Why it matters:

The closing process, where the final payment is made and ownership is transferred, involves signing the Escritura Pública de Compraventa (public deed of sale) in front of a notary. This step requires careful coordination, and any errors can delay or jeopardize the deal.

- What the lawyer does:

Your lawyer will represent you during the closing, review the final documents, and make sure that the transfer of ownership is legally valid. They will also register the property in your name at the Land Registry.

Avoiding Scams and Fraud

- *Why it matters:*

Foreign buyers can sometimes be targets of property scams, such as being sold a property with hidden debts or one that doesn't have legal permits.

- *What the lawyer does:*

A qualified property lawyer will conduct a thorough investigation of the property's history, permits, and compliance with local planning laws. This reduces the risk of buying a property with legal or structural issues that could cost you down the line.

Bilingual Assistance and Clear Communication

- *Why it matters:*

Many legal documents in Spain will be in Spanish, which can create communication barriers if you're unfamiliar with the language. Misinterpretation of legal terms can have serious consequences.

- *What the lawyer does:*

A bilingual lawyer can translate all necessary documents and explain legal jargon clearly, ensuring that you fully understand each step of the process. This clarity is key to making informed decisions.

Representation in Your Absence

- Why it matters:

If you are not based in Spain full-time, managing the purchase remotely can be challenging. A local lawyer can act on your behalf, ensuring the transaction continues smoothly even if you are abroad.

- What the lawyer does:

You can grant your lawyer Power of Attorney (Poder Notarial), enabling them to handle various legal procedures, such as signing contracts and making payments, in your absence.

Setting Up Your New Life

- Arranging for Transportation: Airports and Travel

Setting up transportation in Spain can vary depending on your region and specific needs. Whether you are commuting for work, planning to explore various regions, or making business trips, Spain offers an efficient transportation network, including car hire, extensive train services, and several major airports. Here's an overview of how to organize transportation across the country:

Car Hire in Spain

- Best for Flexibility:

Hiring a car is the most convenient option for exploring Spain's more rural areas and small towns that are less accessible by public transport. Spain is full of charming villages, national parks, and beaches that are often easier to reach by car.

- *Where to Hire:*

Car hire is available in most cities and towns, and at major airports. Popular rental companies include Hertz, Avis, Europcar, and local firms. Larger cities like Madrid, Barcelona, Seville, and Málaga have many car hire options.

- *Tips for Car Hire:*

- Book in advance to secure lower rates, especially during peak seasons.

- Full insurance is worth considering, particularly if you plan to drive in mountainous areas or older parts of cities with narrow streets.

- *Parking:*

Be cautious in cities like Madrid, Barcelona, and Seville, where parking can be expensive and limited. Look for accommodations with parking or use public garages.

- *Driving restrictions:*

Be aware of low-emission zones (Zonas de Bajas Emisiones) in major cities, where access may be restricted or require special permits for certain vehicles.

- *Toll Roads:*

Some major highways (Autopistas) in Spain have tolls, so plan accordingly.

Train Services in Spain

- High-speed Trains (AVE):

Spain has an extensive high-speed rail network (AVE), which connects major cities efficiently. AVE trains can whisk you between cities like Madrid, Barcelona, Seville, Valencia, and Málaga at speeds up to 310 km/h (193 mph).

- Example Travel Times:

Madrid to Barcelona takes about 2.5 hours by AVE, while Madrid to Seville takes about 2 hours and 30 minutes.

- Medium and Long-Distance Trains:

Regional trains, such as Renfe's Media Distancia and Larga Distancia, connect smaller towns and cities across the country. While slower, they are often the best option for less urban areas like northern Spain or interior towns.

- Tips for Using Trains:

- Book in advance:

AVE tickets can be cheaper when booked ahead of time, especially if you find special discounts or promotions on the Renfe website.

- Consider travel passes:

The Renfe Spain Pass is a great option if you plan to travel frequently between cities over a short period. It offers flexible and discounted travel.

Spain unlocked an expat's key to the real estate market.

- *Regional train schedules:*

Check timetables, especially during weekends or holidays, as services may be limited.

Proximity of Airports

Spain is well-connected by air, with numerous international and domestic airports. Depending on where you live or your travel needs, you'll likely find one of the following airports most convenient:

- Major Airports in Spain:

- Madrid-Barajas Airport (MAD):

Spain's busiest airport, with flights to cities worldwide. Convenient for residents of Madrid, central Spain, and northern regions.

- Barcelona-El Prat Airport (BCN):

Serving northeastern Spain, it's the second-largest airport, with frequent flights across Europe and globally.

- Málaga-Costa del Sol Airport (AGP):

Key for travelers in southern Spain and the Costa del Sol region, with a wide range of domestic and international flights.

- Valencia Airport (VLC):

Serves the eastern coast, including Valencia and surrounding areas.

- *Seville Airport (SVQ):*

Convenient for western Andalucía and nearby regions like Extremadura.

- *Bilbao Airport (BIO):*

The main gateway to northern Spain, especially the Basque Country.

- *Palma de Mallorca Airport (PMI):*

One of Spain's busiest airports, primarily serving the Balearic Islands.

- *Alicante-Elche Airport (ALC):*

A popular hub for the Costa Blanca region, with many flights from the UK and other European destinations.

- Airport Transfers:

- *Public Transport:*

Many airports offer direct train or bus connections to city centers. For example, Madrid and Barcelona airports have metro and train services, while Málaga has a commuter train linking the airport to the city center.

- *Taxis and Rideshare:*

Taxis are widely available at all airports, and rideshare apps like Uber and Cabify operate in many cities.

- *Car hire:*

All major airports have car rental facilities, making it easy to pick up a vehicle upon arrival.

Spain unlocked an expat's key to the real estate market.

Bus Services in Spain

- Long-Distance Coaches:

Buses are a popular and affordable way to travel between cities and towns in Spain. Companies like ALSA, Avanza, and FlixBus offer extensive networks. Buses tend to be more affordable than trains, though travel times can be longer.

- Intercity and Local Buses:

Each major city has its own local bus network, such as EMT in Madrid and Barcelona's TMB. These networks are efficient for getting around urban areas.

- Tips for Bus Travel:

- Online booking:

Many long-distance bus companies allow you to book tickets online, often at discounted rates.

- Bus apps:

Download apps like Moovit or the operator's app for live updates on routes and schedules.

Urban Public Transport

- Metro:

Madrid and Barcelona have large metro systems, making them the best option for getting around these cities quickly. Valencia and Bilbao also have metro services.

Spain unlocked an expat's key to the real estate market.

- *Trams:*

Cities like Zaragoza, Alicante, and Seville have tram networks that are perfect for short, inner-city trips.

- *Commuter Trains (Cercanías):*

Spain's commuter trains, called Cercanías, connect suburbs to city centers.

Madrid, Barcelona, Seville, and Valencia have the most extensive Cercanías networks.

- Tips for Public Transport:

- *Pre-paid travel cards:*

Many cities have travel cards, like Madrid's Tarjeta Multi or Barcelona's T-Casual, which offer discounted fares for buses, trams, and metros.

- *Real-time apps:*

Use public transport apps to get real-time updates on arrival times and delays.

- Health Care: Hospitals, Doctors, and Insurance

Provide insights into Spain's health care system, how expats can access public and private health care, and the importance of health insurance.

- Education: Schools and Local Resources

Outline the education options available to expats, including international schools, local Spanish schools, and bilingual programs.

Spain unlocked an expat's key to the real estate market.

- Language Barriers: Overcoming Communication Challenges

Share tips on overcoming language barriers, whether through learning Spanish, using translation apps, or enrolling in language courses.

Living in Spain

- Integrating into the Community: Tips for Expats

Integrating into a new community in Spain, whether you've moved for work, retirement, or a lifestyle change, can enrich your experience and make your stay more fulfilling. Spain has a warm, welcoming culture, but it can take time to feel truly integrated, especially if you are unfamiliar with the language or local customs. Here are some practical tips to help you become part of the local community:

Join Expat and Local Groups

- *Expat Communities:*

Connecting with fellow expats is a great first step. Many cities and regions in Spain have active expat communities where you can find support, advice, and social activities. Popular places for expat groups include:

- *Costa del Sol (Málaga, Marbella, Nerja):*

A hotspot for British, German, and Scandinavian expats.

- *Madrid and Barcelona:*

Both cities have large, diverse expat populations, with plenty of meetups, clubs, and activities for newcomers.

- *Valencia and Alicante:*

Growing expat communities, particularly among English-speaking residents.

- *Online Platforms:*

Websites like Meetup.com and InterNations and costawomen.com have local groups across Spain that organise events, from language exchanges, business clubs, friendly meet ups to hiking trips. Facebook also has many city-specific expat groups where you can get local recommendations or join activities. Property in Spain for sale is a good start.

- *Local Interest Groups:*

To connect with Spaniards, seek out local clubs and hobby groups that interest you. These could include:

- Sports clubs (e.g., tennis, cycling, paddle tennis, football)

- Cooking or dance classes (e.g., flamenco, salsa, or learning how to cook paella)

- Language exchange groups (called "intercambios"), where you can practice Spanish while helping locals improve their English.

- Cultural associations: Many townhalls and cities have associations dedicated to preserving local traditions or promoting cultural activities. Joining a local choir, theatre group, or art collective can help you meet people and engage with the culture. They usually have a website and Facebook page sometimes in different languages.

Spain unlocked an expat's key to the real estate market.

Learn Spanish (or the Local Language)

- Language Courses:

While you can get by in many areas of Spain with English, learning Spanish will significantly deepen your experience and ability to connect with locals. In regions like Catalonia, Galicia, or the Basque Country, knowing some Catalan, Galician, or Basque is also appreciated.

- Formal classes:

You can find language courses in local universities, community centers, or private language schools. Some even offer free or affordable lessons for foreigners.

- Language Exchange:

Participating in language exchanges (intercambios) is an informal way to improve your Spanish. Bars, cafés, and cultural centers often host these events where locals and expats practice languages over a coffee or a drink.

- Tips for Language Learning:

- Be patient with yourself:

Language learning takes time, but locals generally appreciate the effort you make, even if your Spanish isn't perfect.

- Practice daily:

to incorporate Spanish into your daily life, whether it's through conversations with neighbors, watching local TV, or listening to Spanish music.

Participate in Local Festivals and Events

Spain is famous for its lively fiestas and cultural festivals, which are deeply rooted in local traditions and community spirit. Attending or participating in these events is one of the best ways to feel like part of the community.

- *Fiestas and Ferias:*

Every town in Spain has its own patron saint festival (fiestas patronales), where locals gather for days of celebration, music, and food. Key festivals include:

- *Semana Santa (Holy Week):*

Held in cities like Seville and Málaga, this religious festival involves large processions and is a key cultural event.

- *Feria de Abril (April Fair) in Seville:*

A massive spring fair full of dancing, music, and traditional costumes.

- *Las Fallas in Valencia:*

A fiery celebration in March involving elaborate sculptures, fireworks, and parades.

- *San Fermín in Pamplona:*

Known for the Running of the Bulls, this festival is famous worldwide.

- *Local Fairs and Harvest Festivals:*

Smaller towns often have ferias, celebrating local products like wine, olives, or seafood. These fairs give you a chance to enjoy local food, participate in traditional dances, and bond with your neighbours.

- Tips for Festivals:

- *Dress the part:*

Locals often wear traditional attire during certain festivals, like flamenco dresses during feria. Dressing up can make you feel more involved.

- *Volunteer:*

Many festivals need volunteers to help with organising, setting up, or assisting visitors, which can also help you meet new people.

4. Volunteer in Your Local Community

Volunteering is an excellent way to integrate into Spanish life, especially if you're looking to give back to the community and make deeper connections. Spain offers various volunteer opportunities in different sectors:

- *Charitable Organisations:*

Join local charities that support social causes like helping the homeless, animal rescue, or supporting the elderly. For example:

- *Cruz Roja (Red Cross):*

Offers volunteering opportunities across Spain in areas like disaster relief, social services, and community support.

- *Food Banks (Bancos de Alimentos):*

Help distribute food to families in need, especially in cities like Madrid, Barcelona, and Valencia.

- *Animal Shelters:*

Many expats volunteer in shelters, especially in rural areas or on the islands, where stray animals are more common.

- *Cultural Volunteering:*

Some cultural and heritage organizations accept volunteers to help with local events, guide tours, or assist with museum activities. This is a great way to meet locals and learn about Spain's history and traditions.

- *Environmental Volunteering:*

Spain's diverse landscapes offer opportunities to participate in conservation efforts, such as beach cleanups, reforestation projects, or wildlife protection, especially in regions like Andalucía, the Canary Islands, and the Pyrenees.

Get Involved in Local Politics and Associations

- *Neighborhood Associations (Asociaciones de Vecinos):*

Many neighborhoods have associations that organize activities, handle local issues, and offer a platform for residents to voice concerns. Attending meetings or volunteering for these groups is a great way to get to know your neighbors and contribute to your area.

Spain unlocked an expat's key to the real estate market.

- *Municipal Events:*

Attend town hall meetings, community workshops, or local council events to better understand how your local area functions and how you can be involved.

Support Local Businesses and Markets

Shopping at local markets and frequenting neighbourhood businesses is another way to become part of the community. Markets in Spain, known as mercados, are hubs of social life, where people come together to buy fresh produce, meat, and fish. Regular visits can help you build relationships with local vendors and neighbours.

- Navigating Local Culture and Customs

When moving to Spain as an expat, it's important to understand key cultural differences, customs, and social etiquette to help you integrate more smoothly. From dining habits to daily routines, Spain has its unique rhythm of life that may differ from what expats are used to. Here are some key areas to consider:

Dining Habits

- *Mealtimes:*

Spanish people eat later than in many other countries. Lunch (the main meal of the day) is typically served between 2:00 and 3:30 p.m., while dinner often doesn't start until 9:00 or 10:00 p.m.

Spain unlocked an expat's key to the real estate market.

- *Pace of Meals:*

Meals, especially lunch and dinner, are social events and often take longer. It's normal to linger over food, with multiple courses served slowly, often accompanied by wine.

- *Tipping:*

Tipping is less common and less expected than in countries like the U.S. A small tip (5-10%) or rounding up the bill is generally sufficient in restaurants.

- *Tapas Culture:*

Tapas are small dishes served with drinks, especially in bars. Sharing plates and enjoying a variety of small bites is common, and it's more of a casual, social experience rather than a sit-down meal.

Siesta and Business Hours

- *Siesta Time:*

Traditionally, many businesses (especially outside big cities) close for a siesta between 2:00 and 5:00 p.m. However, large urban areas are moving away from this practice, and many businesses may remain open, especially in the hospitality and retail sectors.

- *Business Hours:*

Shops often open from 10:00 a.m. to 1:30 or 2:00 p.m., then close for siesta, and reopen from 5:00 p.m. to 8:00 or 9:00 p.m.

Banks, offices, and government buildings typically operate from 8:30 a.m. to 2:30 p.m.

Social Etiquette

- Greetings:

Spaniards greet each other with a kiss on both cheeks (starting with the right cheek). This is common among women and between women and men in social settings. Men often greet each other with a handshake or hug.

- Personal Space:

People tend to stand closer during conversations, and physical touch (like a pat on the arm or back) is more common than in some other cultures. Interruptions during conversations are more accepted as a sign of engagement.

- Titles and Formality:

While Spain has a relatively informal social culture, using Señor/Señora (Mr./Mrs.) followed by the last name shows respect in formal or professional situations. It's also customary to greet with a polite "Buenos días" (Good morning) or "Buenas tardes" (Good afternoon) when entering shops, offices, or homes.

Family and Social Life

- Family-Oriented Society:

Spain is highly family-oriented, and it's common for multiple generations to live close together or gather frequently. Family meals and weekend gatherings are important.

Spain unlocked an expat's key to the real estate market.

- *Socialising in Public:*

Spaniards enjoy socialising outside the home, often meeting in bars or restaurants rather than hosting guests at home. The plaza (town square) is a popular gathering spot.

- *Festivals and Holidays:*

Spain has numerous local festivals (known as fiestas), and many towns and regions celebrate their own unique traditions. It's important to be aware of local holidays, as businesses may close, and traffic can increase.

Time Perception

- *Punctuality:*

Spaniards are generally more relaxed about punctuality, especially in social situations. Being 10-15 minutes late to a social event is often acceptable, though it's still good to be on time for business meetings.

- *"Mañana" Culture:*

The idea of "mañana" (literally meaning "tomorrow") refers to a more laid-back attitude towards deadlines and urgency. It's not uncommon for things to happen at a slower pace than in some countries, particularly in the bureaucratic or construction sectors.

Spain unlocked an expat's key to the real estate market.

Work-Life Balance

- Work to Live:

Spaniards place great value on leisure and quality of life. The emphasis is often on "working to live," not "living to work." As a result, you'll find many people taking long lunch breaks, enjoying a good work-life balance, and leaving work on time.

- Long Holidays:

August is a common vacation month when many businesses close or slow down, as locals take extended summer holidays.

Language

- Spanish Language:

While English is spoken in tourist areas, learning basic Spanish will greatly enhance your experience, especially in smaller towns. In some regions, you may also encounter regional languages like Catalan, Basque, or Galician.

- Politeness:

Spaniards appreciate politeness. Using por favor" (please), "gracias"(thank you), and "disculpa"(excuse me) in daily interactions shows respect.

Driving and Public Transport

- Driving Etiquette:

Spaniards are assertive drivers, and it's common to see more aggressive driving behaviours, especially in larger cities. However, driving in rural areas is more relaxed.

- *Public Transport:*

Public transportation is well-developed, especially in cities. Buses, trams, and trains are widely used and punctual, though expect busy times during the siesta or evening rush.

- Pets and Animals: Bringing Your Furry Friends

Bringing pets to Spain involves several steps, including ensuring that your pet meets the necessary vaccination, identification, and health requirements, as well as finding pet-friendly housing and understanding local regulations. Here's an outline of the process:

Microchip and Identification

- *Microchip:*

Your pet must be microchipped with an ISO-compliant 15-digit microchip. The microchip should be implanted before your pet's rabies vaccination.

-*Pet Passport:*

If you are bringing your pet from within the EU, they will need a European Pet Passport issued by a licensed vet. For non-EU countries, a third-country veterinary certificate is required.

Vaccination Requirements

- *Rabies Vaccination:*

Pets must be vaccinated against rabies. The vaccination should be given at least 21 days before travel but not more than 12 months before entry. If the pet is coming from a country outside the EU or a high-risk rabies country, a rabies titer test may also be required, showing that your pet has sufficient antibodies.

- *Other Vaccinations:*

While not always mandatory, it's recommended to ensure your pet is up to date on common vaccinations like distemper, parvovirus, and hepatitis.

Health Certificate

- *Veterinary Health Certificate:*

This certificate must be issued by a licensed veterinarian within 10 days of travel. It confirms that your pet is healthy and fit for travel.

- *Non-EU Pets:*

For pets traveling from non-EU countries, the certificate must be endorsed by the relevant official veterinary authority in your country.

Transporting Your Pet

- *Air Travel:*

If flying, check with the airline for specific regulations regarding pet travel. Some airlines allow pets in the cabin, while others may require them to travel in the cargo hold, depending on their size and weight.

- *Pet Carrier:*

Ensure your pet is comfortable and secure in an IATA-approved carrier.

Spain unlocked an expat's key to the real estate market.

Entering Spain

- Point of Entry:

Upon arrival in Spain, customs officials may ask to see your pet's paperwork, including the health certificate, vaccination records, and microchip information.

- Customs Declaration:

If your pet is traveling as cargo or accompanied luggage, you may need to declare them at customs.

Quarantine

- Pets traveling from most countries, including EU member states and many non-EU countries with similar rabies controls, do not require quarantine. However, pets from high-risk countries may be subject to further scrutiny.

Navigating Pet-Friendly Housing in Spain

- Finding Pet-Friendly Accommodation:

When renting a house or apartment in Spain, make sure to clarify with landlords if pets are allowed. It's common for landlords to ask for an additional deposit if you have pets. Websites like Idealista and Fotocasa often have filters to search specifically for pet-friendly properties.

- Pet Ownership Rules: Some residential communities (urbanizaciones) may have specific rules about pets, such as breed restrictions, leash laws, or limits on the number of pets allowed.

Accessing Pet-Friendly Areas

- Parks and Public Spaces:

Spain is generally pet-friendly, with many cities offering designated dog parks and even some dog-friendly beaches (e.g., Playa de la Rubina in Catalonia or Playa Canina in Málaga). However, pets are typically required to be on a leash in public areas.

- Restaurants and Cafés:

Some restaurants and cafés, especially those with outdoor seating, allow dogs. It's always best to ask beforehand.

- Public Transport:

Small pets can travel on public transport (trains, buses) if they are in a carrier. Larger pets may be subject to additional rules depending on the city or transport company.

Other Considerations

- Pet Insurance:

While not mandatory, pet insurance is recommended to cover any potential vet costs or liability in case of accidents.

- Veterinary Services:

Spain has many qualified veterinarians, especially in urban areas. Make sure to register your pet with a local vet soon after arrival for any checkups or required vaccinations.

Empadronamiento: Register with local authorities.

The empadronamiento is the process of registering with the local town hall (ayuntamiento) in Spain. This registration

Spain unlocked an expat's key to the real estate market.

officially records your residency in a particular municipality, providing several benefits and sometimes required for specific formalities.

Here's why empadronamiento is important:

1. Proof of Residency:It serves as proof that you reside in Spain, which can be essential for applying for certain permits, registering for public healthcare, or enrolling children in school.

2. Access to Public Services: Many municipal services require proof of empadronamiento, including access to local health services, discounts on public transport, and other social benefits.

3. Voting Rights: For EU nationals, empadronamiento may allow you to vote in local elections.

4. Legal Compliance: Registering helps authorities keep an accurate count of residents, which can impact local funding and resource distribution.

The registration process generally involves providing identification, proof of address, and sometimes a completed application form. Once registered, you receive a certificate (Certificado de Empadronamiento) that you may need to update if you move within or to a different municipality.

The Tarjeta de Identidad de Extranjero (TIE)

A mandatory identification card for non-EU nationals residing in Spain for more than six months. This card is essential for proving your legal residency in Spain and includes your

Número de Identidad de Extranjero (NIE), a unique tax and identification number. Here's an overview of the TIE application process:

Steps for Applying for a TIE

1. Gather Necessary Documents:

   - Valid passport (original and photocopy)

   - Proof of residence (such as your empadronamiento)

   - Proof of legal residency authorisation (such as a visa or residence permit)

   - Two recent passport-sized photos

   - Payment receipt of the application fee (modelo 790 código 012 form)

   - Completed EX-17 application form for TIE

You can download the application forms for the TIE (Tarjeta de Identidad de Extranjero) from the Spanish government's official website:

Form EX-17 (Application for the TIE card)

https://extranjeros.inclusion.gob.es/es/modelossolicitudes/mod_solicitudes2/index.html

On this page, look for Formulario EX-17 under "Tarjeta de Identidad de Extranjero" and download the PDF version.

Also, you need Form 790 (Code 012) to pay the associated fee:

Spain unlocked an expat's key to the real estate market.

https://sede.policia.gob.es/Tasa790_012/

Make sure to fill out both forms and bring them, along with any required documents, to your TIE appointment. The form is downloadable in PDF format. You can fill it out electronically or print it and complete it by hand. Ensure that all fields are completed accurately to avoid delays in processing.

2. Schedule an Appointment: Appointments are required and can be booked online through the Spanish government's Cita Previa system. It's recommended to schedule this early due to high demand in many regions. To make an online appointment for a TIE (Tarjeta de Identidad de Extranjero) in Spain, you can visit the official appointment website:

https://sede.administracionespublicas.gob.es/icpplus

Go to the website, Select your province. Choose the procedure: "Policía - Certificados UE" or "Expedición de tarjeta de identidad de extranjero."

Follow the steps to enter your personal information, select a date, and confirm the appointment.

Make sure to have all the necessary documents ready before your appointment.

3. Attend the Appointment: Bring all documents to your local Oficina de Extranjería (immigration office) on the scheduled date. During this appointment, your fingerprints will be taken, and your application will be reviewed.

4. Collect Your TIE: After a few weeks, you'll receive a notification to collect your TIE card. Typically, you must pick it up in person at the same immigration office.

Important Notes

Timeliness: You should apply for a TIE within 30 days of entering Spain.

Validity: The TIE's validity period depends on your residence permit type and may need renewal if you extend your stay.

Renewal: If renewing, you'll follow a similar process but should start before the current TIE expires to avoid any legal complications.

The TIE card serves as your primary ID in Spain, streamlining access to services, banking, healthcare, and more.

Selling Your Property

- The Selling Process: From Listing to Closing

Selling property in Spain involves several key steps, from finding a reliable real estate agent to negotiating offers and closing the sale. Here's a breakdown of the process:

1. Finding a Real Estate Agent

- Research:

It's advisable to start by finding a reputable real estate agent, particularly one experienced in the local market and familiar with your type of property (residential, holiday, or commercial).

- *Check Credentials:*

Verify that the agent is registered with a professional body (e.g., API - Agente de la Propiedad Inmobiliaria) and has good reviews from other sellers.

- *Agree on Terms:*

The agent's commission typically ranges from **3% to 6%** of the sale price. Make sure to clarify their fee, the services provided (e.g., marketing, property viewings, legal support), and whether you'll sign an **exclusive** or **non-exclusive** contract.

2. Preparing the Property for Sale

- *Valuation:*

Your agent will help you set a realistic price by conducting a market analysis of similar properties in the area. Some sellers opt for a professional valuation.

- *Legal Documentation:*

Ensure all necessary legal documents are in order:

- *Title deed (Escritura):*

Proving your ownership of the property.

- *Energy Performance Certificate (Certificado de Eficiencia Energética):*

Mandatory for selling a property.

- *Habitability Certificate (Cédula de Habitabilidad):*

May be required in some regions, especially for older properties.

Spain unlocked an expat's key to the real estate market.

- *IBI receipt (Impuesto sobre Bienes Inmuebles):*

A tax receipt showing that property taxes are up to date.

- Property Presentation:

Clean, declutter, and stage your property to make it more appealing to buyers. Professional photography and possibly virtual tours may also be organized by your agent.

3. Marketing the Property

- *Listings and Advertising:*

The real estate agent will have a marketing plan for your particular property and list the property on popular property portals e.g., Idealista, Fotocasa, Rightmove and other platforms, targeting both domestic and international buyers. They will share the property on an MLS website with 1000s of other agents. Use social media channels to promote the property to target audiences.

- *Signage:*

It's common to place a "For Sale" sign on the property, especially in residential areas.

- *Open Houses & Viewings:*

The agent will schedule property viewings with potential buyers. If you live abroad, the agent may handle these entirely on your behalf.

Receiving Offers and Negotiating

- Receiving Offers:

Once interested buyers make offers, your agent will communicate them to you. Be prepared to negotiate the price, especially if the market is competitive.

- Buyer Due Diligence:

It's important to ensure the buyer is financially capable of purchasing the property. Many buyers in Spain need mortgage approval, and you may ask for a proof of funds or mortgage pre-approval.

- Negotiation:

When negotiating, discuss not just the price but also the terms of the sale, such as whether certain furniture or fixtures are included, timelines, or any contingencies the buyer may have.

Signing the Reservation Agreement (Contrato de Reserva)

- Reservation Deposit:

Once you accept an offer, the buyer typically places a small deposit (usually around €3,000 to €6,000) to reserve the property. This deposit confirms their intention to purchase and takes the property off the market.

- Reservation Agreement:

This document outlines basic details of the sale (price, buyer's and seller's names, property details) and serves as a prelude to the formal contracts.

Signing the Private Purchase Contract (Contrato de Arras)

- Down Payment:

This is the formal purchase contract, which the seller and buyer sign. At this stage, the buyer usually pays a deposit of 10% of the agreed sale price

- Non-Refundable Clause:

The deposit is non-refundable if the buyer pulls out, but if the seller pulls out, they usually owe the buyer double the deposit as compensation.

- Contract Terms:

This contract includes the sale price, the deposit amount, the completion date, and any other terms agreed upon.

Final Legal and Financial Preparations

- Notary Appointment:

The property sale in Spain must be formalized in front of a notary. You'll need to schedule this with your agent or solicitor.

- Legal Checks:

Your solicitor will ensure there are no outstanding debts, liens, or issues with the property (e.g., unpaid utility bills, community fees) before the sale can proceed.

- Tax Obligations:

As the seller, you may have to pay taxes on the sale, including:

- *Capital Gains Tax (Impuesto sobre la Renta de No Residentes):*

Applies to non-resident sellers (19% for EU/EEA citizens, 24% for non-EU citizens) on any profit from the sale.

- *Plusvalía Tax:*

A local tax based on the increase in the value of the land on which the property sits.

Closing the Sale

- *Completion at the Notary:*

On the agreed completion date, you, the buyer, and your legal representatives meet at the notary's office. The notary reviews all documents and ensures the sale is legally binding.

- *Signing the Escritura (Title Deed):*

Both parties sign the new title deed, transferring ownership of the property to the buyer.

- *Final Payment:*

The buyer pays the remaining balance of the purchase price (usually via bank transfer or certified check), and you hand over the keys.

- *Notary Fees and Costs:*

While the buyer typically pays most notary fees, make sure you are aware of any seller obligations or shared costs.

Spain unlocked an expat's key to the real estate market.

Post-Sale Responsibilities

- Taxes and Settlements:

Settle any final utility bills or community fees associated with the property.

- Non-Resident Capital Gains Retention:

If you're a non-resident, 3% of the sale price may be retained by the Spanish tax authorities as a withholding to cover potential capital gains taxes.

Final Checklist:

- Ensure that all taxes and fees are paid (like the Plusvalía tax).

- Notify utility companies and homeowners associations of the change in ownership.

- File any necessary documents with the Spanish tax office, especially for non-residents.

- Selling Costs: What to Consider

When selling property in Spain, you'll need to factor in several costs that can significantly impact the proceeds from the sale. These include taxes, agent fees, legal expenses, and other miscellaneous charges. Here's a breakdown of the typical costs involved:

Real Estate Agent Fees

- Commission:

Real estate agents in Spain typically charge 3% to 6% of the final sale price (plus VAT at 21%). This fee is generally agreed upon before the sale and can be higher or lower depending on the agent and the region.

Capital Gains Tax (CGT)

- For Residents: If you're a tax resident in Spain, the capital gains tax applies to any profit made from the sale of your property. The rates for residents are:

  - 19% on gains up to €6,000.

  - 21% on gains between €6,001 and €50,000.

  - 23% on gains above €50,000.

- For Non-Residents: Non-resident sellers pay a flat 19% tax on the profit if they are EU/EEA citizens. For non-EU/EEA citizens, the rate is 24%.

- Exemptions for Residents:

  - Over 65 years old and selling your primary residence: you may be exempt if you've lived in the property for at least three years.

  - Reinvestment Exemption: If you reinvest the proceeds in another main residence within two years, you might avoid CGT (applicable only for tax residents).

- Example: If you bought a property for €200,000 and sold it for €300,000, your gain is €100,000. If you are a resident, the CGT on the first €6,000 is 19%, on the next €44,000 is 21%, and the remaining €50,000 is taxed at 23%.

Plusvalía Tax (Municipal Capital Gains Tax)

- *What It Is:*

The Plusvalía is a local tax charged on the increase in the value of the land (not the building) since you purchased the property. It is calculated based on the cadastral value of the land and the number of years you've owned the property.

- *Who Pays:*

While the seller usually pays this tax, it can sometimes be negotiated with the buyer.

- Example:

If the cadastral value of your land is €50,000 and you've owned the property for 10 years, your Plusvalía might range from €500 to €3,000, depending on the municipality and the rate applied.

Non-Resident Withholding Tax

- *What It Is:*

If you're a non-resident, the Spanish tax authorities withhold 3% of the sale price to cover potential capital gains tax liabilities. This amount is retained by the buyer and paid directly to the tax office on your behalf.

- *Refund:*

If your actual capital gains tax liability is less than the 3% withheld, you can claim a refund of the difference, though this process can take several months.

Spain unlocked an expat's key to the real estate market.

- *Example:*

On a sale price of €300,000, the withholding amount will be €9,000

Legal Fees

- *Solicitor Fees:*

It's highly recommended to hire a solicitor (abogado) to handle the legal aspects of the sale, especially for non-resident sellers. Fees generally range from 1% to 1.5% of the sale price.

- Example:

For a €300,000 property, the legal fees would range between €3,000 and €4,500, depending on the complexity of the sale.

Notary and Registry Fees

- *Notary Fees:*

While notary fees are often the buyer's responsibility, some costs might be shared. These fees typically range between €600 and €1,000, depending on the sale price and the complexity of the transaction.

- *Land Registry Fees:*

The buyer typically covers the cost of registering the sale, but some sellers may contribute to these fees as well. The cost for registering a property usually ranges from €400 to €650

Mortgage Cancellation Fees (If Applicable)

- Early Repayment Fees:

If you have an outstanding mortgage on the property, there may be early repayment or cancellation fees. These are typically 0.5% to 1% of the remaining mortgage balance, though this varies by lender.

- Mortgage Cancellation at Notary:

Officially canceling the mortgage at the notary can cost €600 to €1,000

- Example:

If you have €100,000 remaining on your mortgage and an early repayment fee of 1%, you would pay €1,000 plus notary fees.

Energy Performance Certificate (EPC)

- What It Is:

This certificate is mandatory when selling a property in Spain. It measures the property's energy efficiency and is valid for 10 years.

- Cost:

The cost of obtaining an EPC typically ranges from €100 to €400, depending on the size and location of the property.

Miscellaneous Costs

- Property Presentation and Repairs:

Some sellers choose to make minor repairs, repaint, or stage their property to make it more appealing to buyers. These costs vary depending on what improvements are made.

- Property Clearance:

If the property is fully furnished, you may need to cover the cost of clearing or moving furniture and belongings. This can range from a few hundred euros for basic clearance to more for larger properties.

Example Cost Breakdown for a €300,000 Sale (Non-Resident)

- Real Estate Agent Fees (5%): €15,000 + VAT (€18,150 total)

- Capital Gains Tax (19%) on €100,000 profit: €19,000

- Plusvalía Tax: €1,500 (estimated)

- Legal Fees (1%): €3,000

- Notary Fees: €800

- Mortgage Cancellation Fees: €1,000 (if applicable)

- Energy Performance Certificate: €200

-Non-Resident Withholding Tax (3% of sale price): €9,000 (refundable if no capital gain)

Spain unlocked an expat's key to the real estate market.

Why Get a Spanish will?

Getting a will in Spain is a smart move for expats and property owners because it simplifies the inheritance process, reduces legal hurdles, and minimizes costs for heirs. Here's why it's beneficial:

Streamlines Inheritance for Spanish Assets

Spanish inheritance law applies to assets located in Spain, so a Spanish will ensure your property and other assets are distributed according to your wishes within the framework of Spanish law. It clarifies what should happen to assets in Spain, making it easier for heirs to inherit without navigating complex international legal procedures.

Avoids Lengthy Probate Processes

Without a Spanish will, the probate process can take much longer, as foreign wills need to be translated, legalized, and validated by Spanish courts. Having a Spanish will in place allows for a faster, smoother process, often reducing the time required to transfer assets.

In Spain, inheritance rules impose *forced heirship*, meaning certain proportions of your estate may be reserved for direct descendants or close relatives. However, a will can grant you more control over the distribution of the "free disposal" portion of your estate, allowing you to allocate assets according to your wishes.

Having a clear will can also aid heirs in preparing for and potentially minimizing inheritance tax. Each Spanish region has different inheritance tax rates and allowances, and with a will, heirs can better plan for these taxes.

Without a Spanish will, your assets are distributed according to Spanish intestacy laws, which may not align with your preferences. A Spanish will gives you the opportunity to specify exactly who should receive what, ensuring your assets are passed on in line with your intentions.

Dealing with an estate can be challenging for loved ones, especially when it involves a foreign country's legal system. A Spanish will help your family avoid complications, ensuring the process is more straightforward and minimizing the administrative burden on them.

A Spanish will typically cost around €200 to €500 and can be set up with the help of a Spanish lawyer or notary.

- Preparing Your Home for Sale

Staging your property, making necessary repairs, and marketing it effectively are key to attracting buyers and ensuring a quicker sale at a favourable price. Here are some useful tips for each step:

Property Staging

Staging your property involves preparing it to look its best for potential buyers. It helps create a welcoming atmosphere and allows buyers to envision themselves living in the space.

Declutter and Depersonalise

- Clear out excess items:

Remove personal belongings, family photos, and excessive decor. Keep surfaces clean and simple to make rooms look larger and more inviting.

- Minimize furniture:

Arrange furniture in a way that highlights the room's size and functionality. Remove bulky or unnecessary furniture to make the space feel more open.

- Organise storage spaces:

Buyers will inspect closets and cupboards. Keep them tidy to show off available storage space.

Clean Thoroughly

- Deep clean:

Ensure the entire property is spotless, including bathrooms, kitchen appliances, floors, windows, and outdoor spaces.

- Odor control:

Eliminate any odors (pets, cooking smells, etc.) that could deter buyers. Freshen the air with light, natural scents.

Enhance Lighting

- Maximize natural light:

Open curtains or blinds to let in as much natural light as possible. Clean windows to make spaces brighter.

Spain unlocked an expat's key to the real estate market.

- Supplement with artificial light:

Add floor or table lamps to poorly lit areas. Warm, inviting lighting creates a cozy atmosphere.

Neutralise Color Scheme

- Use neutral tones:

Neutral colors (whites, beiges, grays) make the space feel clean and universally appealing. Consider painting walls in light tones to brighten rooms and make them feel more spacious.

- Add accents:

Use colorful throw pillows, rugs, or artwork to add subtle pops of color without overwhelming the space.

Highlight Key Features

- Accentuate best spaces:

Make sure your property's best features—like a great view, a spacious kitchen, or a charming garden—are shown off.

- Create focal points:

Arrange furniture and decor to draw attention to unique features such as fireplaces, built-in shelves, or large windows.

Outdoor Curb Appeal

- Tidy the garden and entrance:

First impressions matter.

Mow the lawn, trim hedges, and add plants or flowers to make the property more inviting from the outside.

- *Clean the entrance:*

Repaint or clean the front door, add a new welcome mat, and ensure the entryway is welcoming and well-maintained.

Making Necessary Repairs

Before listing your property, take care of any maintenance issues to avoid turning off potential buyers and to help justify your asking price.

Fix Minor Repairs

- *Repair leaky faucets:*

A small leak can give the impression of poor maintenance. Fix any plumbing issues, whether in the kitchen or bathroom.

- *Patch up holes or cracks:*

Fill any holes in walls, repair cracked tiles or fix broken windows.

- *Replace worn-out fixtures:*

Update old or broken light fixtures, cabinet handles, or faucets to give the space a fresh look.

Address Major Repairs

- *Assess major systems:*

Ensure the heating, plumbing, electrical systems, and air conditioning (if applicable) are functioning properly. Buyers often want a property that is move-in ready.

Spain unlocked an expat's key to the real estate market.

- Roof and structural repairs:

If there are roof leaks, structural issues, or foundation problems, these should be addressed before listing the property to avoid major delays in the sale process.

Consider Cosmetic Upgrades

- Repaint key areas:

A fresh coat of paint can make the property look newer and more appealing. Stick to neutral colors to appeal to a wide range of buyers.

- Update kitchen and bathroom:

These rooms are often deal-makers for buyers. Simple updates like new cabinet hardware, light fixtures, or a backsplash can give the room a more modern feel without a full renovation.

Marketing the Home Effectively

Effective marketing will help you reach the right buyers and showcase your property in its best light.

High-Quality Photography

- Professional photography:

Hire a professional photographer to take high-resolution, well-lit photos of your home. Ensure they capture key selling points (natural light, spacious rooms, garden areas, etc.).

- Virtual tours and videos:

Offer virtual tours to allow remote buyers to view your property online. Videos or 360-degree tours can increase interest and engagement, especially for international buyers.

Spain unlocked an expat's key to the real estate market.

Create an Appealing Listing

- Engaging description:

Write a detailed, engaging description of your property. Highlight its unique features (e.g., large garden, proximity to schools, sea view) and nearby amenities (shops, public transport, etc.).

- Accurate information:

Ensure all key information such as square footage, number of bedrooms/bathrooms, and property features is accurate and clearly listed.

Leverage Online Property Portals

- List on top platforms:

Use popular real estate portals like Idealista, Fotocasa, and Rightmove Overseas to reach both local and international buyers.

- Social media promotion:

Share your listing on social media platforms (Facebook, Instagram) and encourage your real estate agent to promote it through their own channels.

Open Houses and Viewings

- Organise open houses:

Depending on your location and the market, an open house can attract multiple buyers at once. Keep the home clean and well-staged for showings.

- Be flexible with viewings:

Allow potential buyers to visit the property at different times of the day and week to accommodate their schedules.

Highlight Special Selling Points

- Focus on location benefits:

Emphasize if the property is located in a desirable area (close to schools, beaches, or public transport).

- Eco-friendly features:

If your property has solar panels or energy-efficient features, make sure these are highlighted as they can attract eco-conscious buyers.

- Turnkey properties:

If the home is move-in ready or partially furnished, this can be a strong selling point for buyers looking for convenience.

Bonus Tip: Competitive Pricing

- Set the right price:

Pricing your property correctly is crucial to attracting buyers. Work with your agent to set a realistic price based on market conditions and comparable properties. Overpricing can lead to a longer selling process, while a competitive price can attract more interest and lead to quicker offers.

- Your Checklist for Moving to Spain

1. Pre-Move Research

- Visit Spain to explore regions.

- Research areas: climate, cost of living, schools, expat communities.

- Learn basic Spanish (or regional languages).

- Research public vs. private healthcare.

- Investigate schools and application processes.

2. Legal Requirements

- Visa Application: Apply for the correct visa (non-EU/EEA citizens).

- NIE Number: Essential for all legal transactions.

- Empadronamiento: Register with local authorities.

- Residence Permit: Apply for TIE (for non-EU citizens).

- Healthcare: Register for public or private health insurance.

3. Financial Planning

- Create a moving budget.

Spain unlocked an expat's key to the real estate market.

- Open a Spanish bank account.

- Understand and plan for Spanish taxes.

- Get Mortgage pre approval.

- Set up currency exchange for large transfers.

- Organise pension transfer (if retiring).

- Set Up a Spanish will.

4. Housing

- Decide to rent or buy

- Hire a real estate agent.

- Understand rental or sales contracts.

- Set up utilities (electricity, water, internet).

5. Settling In

- Register for healthcare.

- Set up utilities and local services.

- Enrol children in schools.

- Start learning or improving Spanish.

- Exchange or apply for a Spanish driver's license.

- Buy or lease a car (if applicable).

6. Building Your New Life

- Join local/expat groups or clubs.

Spain unlocked an expat's key to the real estate market.

- Participate in local festivals and markets.

- Volunteer to engage with the community.

- Stay on top of legal requirements (residency, taxes).

Spain unlocked an expat's key to the real estate market.

Official Government Websites

These official portals will help you manage paperwork, residency, and navigate Spain's bureaucracy.

- Spain's Ministry of Foreign Affairs:

Information on visas, residency permits, and immigration rules for non-EU citizens. Ministry of Foreign Affairs Website

http://www.exteriores.gob.es/

- Expat Rights and Regulations (EU Citizens):

Official portal explaining expat rights, residency, healthcare, and employment for EU citizens. Your Europe Website

https://europa.eu/youreurope/citizens/residence/residence-rights/index_en.htm

- Tax Agency (Agencia Tributaria): The portal for managing taxes, such as registering for NIE Número de Identificación de Extranjeros and paying property taxes. Tax Agency Website

https://www.agenciatributaria.es/

- Seguridad Social:

Spanish Social Security website for health care, pensions, and other benefits. Seguridad Social Website

https://www.seg-social.es/

Spain unlocked an expat's key to the real estate market.

5. Expats Forums and Communities

These forums and platforms allow you to connect with other expats, find local services, and get advice from people already living in Spain.

www.costawomen.com

Expat Forum (Spain Section): A large, active forum where you can ask questions about visas, property, healthcare, and more. Expat Forum Website

https://www.expatforum.com/forums/spain-expat-forum-expats-living-in-spain.81/

InterNations Spain: A social network for expats `*/¡worldwide, with local chapters in most major Spanish cities. Offers meetups and online resources. Inter Nations Website

https://www.internations.org/spain-expats

Spain Expat: A platform providing articles, guides, and a forum specifically for people moving to or living in Spain. Spain Expat Website

https://www.spainexpat.com/

Expatica Spain: Offers news, lifestyle tips, and a forum for expats in Spain. Topics range from visas to parenting to property investment. Expatica Website:

https://www.expatica.com/es/

Spain unlocked an expat's key to the real estate market.

6. Local Services and Directories

Find local businesses, service providers, and professional help with these directories.

Just Landed: A guide for expats covering key areas such as finding a job, property, and services like education and health. Just Landed Website

https://www.justlanded.com/english/Spain

Yellow Pages (Páginas Amarillas):

Spain's directory for finding local businesses, from electricians to doctors. Yellow Pages Website

https://www.paginasamarillas.es/

Ayuntamiento (City Hall) Websites:

Each town or city in Spain has its own official website that provides important information on local services, events, and procedures (e.g., empadronamiento or town registration).

Healthcare Providers and Insurance

Navigating Spain's healthcare system is essential. Public healthcare is available, but many expats also opt for private health insurance.

A leading health insurance provider in Spain, offering comprehensive coverage for expats. Caser Helvetica English Speaking 0034 654091051

Spain unlocked an expat's key to the real estate market.

Schools and Education

For expats with children, finding the right school is crucial.

International schools in Spain cater to expatriates and locals seeking an international education, often with a focus on language and cultural diversity, academic rigor, and pathways to higher education worldwide. Below is a detailed overview of international schools, particularly in popular expat areas like Madrid, Barcelona, the Costa del Sol, and Valencia.

Curriculum Options

- British Curriculum: Many schools offer the British curriculum, leading to GCSEs and A-levels. Examples include King's College (multiple locations) and The British School of Barcelona.

- American Curriculum: Schools like American School of Madrid and American School of Barcelona offer the American High School Diploma and Advanced Placement (AP) programs.

- International Baccalaureate (IB): The IB program is available in several international schools, such as Sotogrande International School on the Costa del Sol, which is known for its strong IB program.

- French, German, and Other National Curricula: French schools, like Lycée Français in Madrid and Barcelona, follow the French national curriculum, while German and Scandinavian schools are also available in larger cities.

Spain unlocked an expat's key to the real estate market.

Locations and Notable Schools

- Madrid:

  - King's College: A prominent British school with strong academic performance, offering the British curriculum.

  - American School of Madrid: Known for its American curriculum and AP offerings, popular among American expats.

  - Lycée Français de Madrid: Offers French curriculum from primary to baccalauréat.

- Barcelona:

  - The British School of Barcelona: Multiple campuses with a British curriculum up to A-levels.

  - Benjamin Franklin International School: Offers American curriculum and IB programs, located in a central area of the city.

  - Lycée Français de Barcelone: Serving the French expat community with a complete French curriculum.

- Costa del Sol (Málaga, Marbella, Sotogrande):

  - Sotogrande International School: IB curriculum from primary to diploma level; popular with diverse international families.

  - Aloha College Marbella: Offers both the British curriculum and the IB Diploma, located in Marbella.

  - Swans International School: British curriculum and an international environment.

Spain unlocked an expat's key to the real estate market.

- Valencia:

    - Caxton College: British curriculum, known for high academic standards, located near Valencia.

    - American School of Valencia: American and IB programs, strong emphasis on multicultural education.

Fees and Admission

- Tuition Fees: International school fees in Spain generally range from €8,000 to €25,000 per year, depending on the location, grade level, and curriculum.

- Madrid and Barcelona: Fees are often on the higher end, with top-tier schools like King's College and American School of Madrid charging between €15,000 and €25,000 annually.

- Costa del Sol and Valencia: Fees tend to be slightly lower, ranging from €8,000 to €20,000. Sotogrande International School, for example, charges around €15,000 to €22,000 annually for the IB Diploma Program.

- Additional Costs: Books, uniforms, transportation, extracurriculars, and meals often add between €1,500 and €3,000 annually. Boarding schools, such as Sotogrande International School, may cost extra for residential facilities.

- Admissions: Most schools require application forms, academic records, and entrance assessments or interviews. Popular schools may have long waiting lists, so early applications are recommended.

Spain unlocked an expat's key to the real estate market.

Unique Offerings and Extracurriculars

- Language Programs: Many international schools offer bilingual or trilingual programs (e.g., Spanish English French or German).

- Sports and Arts: Extracurricular activities like golf, tennis, equestrian sports, and performing arts are common in the Costa del Sol region.

- College Preparation: Schools like American School of Madrid and Sotogrande International School provide college counselling and AP/IB courses, preparing students for universities globally.

This overview captures some key details about international schools in Spain; See below if you need specifics on a particular school or additional areas!

- *International Schools Database:*

Platforms that lists international schools across Spain:

https://www.international-schools-database.com/

https://www.internationalschoolsearch.com/international-schools-in-spain

Spain unlocked an expat's key to the real estate market.

About the Author

NIKKI POWLES

Real estate is My Passion.....

Property in Spain for sale! Working alongside and collaborating with the largest agencies on the Costa Del Sol for the past 25 years.

I, Nikki Powles identified different niches in the Real estate Market and to help address these individual unique market requirements provides you with the relevant help and support throughout the buying process in Spain.

For property Vendors a specially designed marketing plan for each property is provided with stringent follow up procedures and selling strategies unique in the marketplace. Vendors are equally as important to me as my purchasing clients, and I strive to provide all clients with exceptional service levels.

I am the person on the street! As a buyers Agent I can help you avoid the issues and problems with property legalities and non-existent properties that you may encounter because I have the know-how.

I can do the searching for you and provide you with pictures and information straight into your inbox of relevant, available, legal properties ready for you to choose which ones you would like to view. Thus, eliminating any stress or disappointment on your behalf.

Spain unlocked an expat's key to the real estate market.

There is no charge for Buyers. I charge the Vendors typically 5% as a shared Agent or 4% Sole Agent.

My goal is to provide you with all the necessary information, provide you with the tools you need, and guide you through the process to enable you to find your ideal property in Spain making it an exciting and pleasurable experience.

Being bilingual, I can translate for you as we go through the process keeping everything transparent for you.

I can arrange the viewings for you with any of the agents in each area, accompany you to visits and guide you through the whole buying process. There are also many awesome new developments currently in progress that I have full access to view if that is something you are considering.

For detailed information on how I can help you and get the process underway please WhatsApp 0034 654091051 or email info@propertyinspaingroup.com

Other resources and My channels:

For Mortgage information click this link:

https://mortgagedirectsl.com/Nicol.../Mortgage_Direct_Advice

For Currency Exchange information:

https://www.lumonpay.com/referral-new/?F_ID=14365

or https://equalsmoney.com/personal-onboarding?account_id=9131616896

Spain unlocked an expat's key to the real estate market.

My Website: https://propertyinspaingroup.com

Facebook: https://www.facebook.com/profile.php?id=100010589227743

Instagram: https://www.instagram.com/propertyinspaingroup/

X: https://x.com/Nikki_Powles

You Tube: https://www.youtube.com/@propertyinspaingroup

LinkedIn:: www.linkedin.com/in/nikki-powles

TikTok: https://www.tiktok.com/@nikkipowles

Thank you for your interest and please reach out if you need help or assistance. Kind regards Nikki Powles

info@propertyinspaingroup.com

WhatsApp me anytime on 0034 654091051

Disclaimer:

The views and opinions expressed in this book are my personal perspectives and are not intended as professional legal or financial advice. Readers are strongly encouraged to consult with a qualified lawyer or professional for specific guidance related to their circumstances.

This book contains links to my preferred suppliers and affiliates. If you choose to purchase through these links, I may receive a commission at no additional cost to you. These recommendations are based on my personal experience and belief in their quality, but readers should conduct their own due diligence before making any decisions.

Spain unlocked an expat's key to the real estate market.

www.ingramcontent.com/pod-product-compliance
Lightning Source LLC
Chambersburg PA
CBHW071546220526
45469CB00003B/938